The Comeback God

The Comeback God

A Theological Primer for a Life of Faith

EXPLORING CHRISTIAN FAITH

Michael Cooper-White

THE COMEBACK GOD
A Theological Primer for a Life of Faith
Exploring Christian Faith Series

Cover design: Laurie Ingram
Author photo © Melinda Hutton. Used by permission.
Interior design: PerfecType, Nashville, Tenn.

Library of Congress Cataloging-in-Publication Data

Cooper-White, Michael L.
The comeback God : a theological primer for a life of faith / Michael Cooper-White. — Exploring Christian faith.
p. cm.
Includes bibliographical references.
ISBN 978-0-8066-5768-4 (alk. paper)
1. Theology, Doctrinal. I. Title.

BT75.3.C67 2009
230—dc22

2008039857

The paper used in this publication meets the minimum requirements of American National Standard for Information Sciences—Permanence of Paper for Printed Library Materials, ANSI Z329.48-1984.

Manufactured in the U.S.A.

To my family
and to the Gettysburg Seminary community,
I gratefully and humbly dedicate this book.

O come, O come, Emmanuel!

Advent 2008
Michael Cooper-White

Contents

Preface
God Is Coming Back!

THERE IS SOMETHING DEEPLY embedded in our human nature that loves a *comeback*. The word appears in multiple book titles, movies, and television programs (including a series) and is currently the moniker for one of the best-known punk rock bands. A comeback is often associated with a come-from-behind victory in an athletic contest or political campaign. Snatching victory out of the jaws of defeat, or returning to a sport or other activity after an injury or time away, a "comeback kid" is the heroic figure in a host of both real-life and fictional stories. In what has been regarded by some as the ultimate hope for a comeback, baseball legend Ted Williams's body lies in a cryogenic storage facility in Scottsdale, Arizona, awaiting the perfection of technology that will enable his resuscitation for a few more seasons at the plate!

In whatever arena it is experienced or observed, the comeback phenomenon seems to tap into deep wells of human hope and aspiration. Something within us resonates profoundly with the prospect that when all appears lost, there is still a glimmer of hope for a turnaround, a miraculous reversal of fate. Persons who defy dire medical prognoses and survive life-threatening diseases speak of being given back their lives.

The ultimate comeback story of all time is to be found in the testimony of those who first experienced the resurrection of Jesus Christ two days after he was pronounced dead and then buried. "He is risen!" they first whispered privately and later declared publicly. That core proclamation of the gospel, or God's good news, lives on throughout the world two millennia later.

While Jesus' comeback—cosmic in its scope and timeless in its implications—will forever stand as the ultimate victory snatched from deepest death, in a broader sense the entire sweeping history of the triune God's actions and declarations may be understood as a comeback story. The central theme of this short summary of Christian belief and practice is that in response to the deep religious question "Who or what is God?" the clearest and most comprehensive claim is, "God is the cosmic Comeback!"

Beginning in the late 1960s, provocative theologians gained broad public media attention as magazine covers carried bold headlines with their assertions that GOD IS DEAD! As first-year seminarians, our class was assigned an avant-garde book that declared "the good news or glad tidings of the death of God."[1] Along with the death of a divine presence who bore little resemblance to the God of the Bible, these radical theologians called for the demise of the institutional church, inasmuch as "the ecclesiastical tradition has ceased to be Christian, and is now alive only in a demonic and repressive form."[2] Four decades after these radical declarations, God seems to have made a miraculous recovery and once again come back from the divine deathbed! And the church likewise appears to have staged a remarkable comeback, being quite alive and vibrant in some corners of the world—especially among the poor and dispossessed. As I have been privileged to travel about and visit outposts of Christian mission in many places, I have found God's power and presence and the church's bold, courageous witness alive and vigorous.

Any attempt to offer a summary of Christian thought, doctrine, or theology (from Gk. *theos*, "God," + *logos*, "word," literally a "God word") bumps up against the limits of human understanding. The very concept of *God* as a transcendent Being (that is greater than human) points us to a place we can never go in this earthly existence. The Bible and Christian theology assert that human persons are created in the image of God. Yet the "image" in the creature can never fully embrace the Creator any more than my reflection in a mirror can reach out and give my flesh-and-blood self a nice warm hug. Nevertheless, theologians—and that includes all who say or think "God words"—must persist in the effort to say some things about, and even *on behalf of*, God.

In mathematics and the physical sciences, as well as in contemporary practical application, a *vector* represents direction and force, speed, or momentum, without being able to pinpoint exactly where a thing is or to where it may be moving. Pilots flying in crowded airspace are issued "radar vectors" by air traffic controllers. The actual flight path of the aircraft will vary given wind direction and velocity, so a vector only points the plane and pilot in a general direction (away from others in the vicinity). This work of theology seeks to set forth some vectors that point to where God has come from throughout human history, where God may be especially self-revealing in today's world, and where God might be moving in the future. Exactitude in "pinning God down" is never possible. The attempt to do so is always dangerous and leads to rigid judgmental attitudes and ultimately to heresy and unfaith, or to belief in something or someone other than the true living God. "The [Spirit of God, like the] wind blows where it chooses, and you hear the sound of it, but you do not know where it comes from or where it goes" (John 3:8).

Works of theology tend to fall into one of several general types:

- *Biblical theology* attempts to set forth the great truths and teachings of the Holy Scriptures in an organized fashion.

- *Systematic theology* (historically called *dogmatics*, from a Greek word meaning a collection of dogma or correct teachings) organizes itself around overarching themes that define Christian faith. A comprehensive "system" is fashioned from a set of interrelated themes (like a giant skyscraper out of its million construction components).
- *Historical theology* reflects on the sweep of history and how God and God's relationship to the world have been understood at various times by profound thinkers.
- *Pastoral theology* seeks to apply theological themes and theories to actual life situations encountered in the pastoral care of persons within a congregation or other faith community.
- Various manifestations of *liberation theology* (Latin American, Asian, black, feminist, womanist, *mujerista*) take off from the fundamental conviction that God can be found at work liberating oppressed peoples from various forms and forces that imprison them in bondage.
- Newer broad categories of theology include *narrative theology*, which recognizes that the nature of God's interactions with the creation creates a complex web of stories, including our own personal stories; and *constructive theology*, which, while treating many of the themes included in a classic systematic approach, is "determined to keep faith vitally connected to the present-day world and its pressing concerns."[3]

This is a work that does not fall neatly into any of these categories but embraces all of them in some measure. My intent is to construct a biblically based introductory theology with liberating ethical and pastoral possibilities. It is written primarily for lay theologians (including beginning theology students) in recognition of my conviction that, while professors and the clergy play an invaluable teaching role within the church, it is the *laos* (Greek for "people") of God—whose daily callings are not within the academy or institutional church—who constitute the greater part of God's mighty comeback movement.

While I write from the perspective of a lifelong Lutheran and will accordingly draw extensively from the rich wells of my tradition, the hope is that this book will serve as a broadly *ecumenical* (from Gk. *oikomenei*, "household") theology for a wide spectrum of the Christian household. As the great Swiss theologian Karl Barth insisted repeatedly, any theology worth its salt is *churchly or community theology*—it belongs to the entire faith community and not to any individual or tradition. "Like the pendulum which regulates the movements of a clock," wrote Barth, "so theology is responsible for the reasonable service of the community."[4]

The book is organized along fairly conventional lines, treating sequentially key themes that are addressed in most works of systematic theology. Unlike the majority of such introductions, however, the typical order in which the chapter on "final things" comes last is reversed. We will begin reflecting on the end-times and then work backward as it were to creation. A chapter on understanding the current context and how God appears to self-disclose in our midst is followed by one on how the Bible or Holy Scripture is the primary source for theological reflection. The ensuing five sections on great themes of the faith lead to a final chapter on Christian ethics, followed by my personal postscript. For the highly motivated reader, an appendix treats the somewhat esoteric, but important and intriguing, topic of "theological method," or the various ways by which theologians approach their work. Being self-aware of how one goes about any endeavor is critical in understanding strengths and potential contributions, as well as weaknesses and possible blind spots.

God always keeps coming back! God is the irresistible, unstoppable, unremitting force of love, redemption, and renewal in the universe—at all times and in all places. That is the overarching thematic strain that will be played over and over again throughout this short book of theology. And God comes back most especially to those who, from a vantage point of feeble faith, yearn deeply to experience the divine presence. While classic Christian faith teaches that God is surely always and everywhere present, the testimonies of innumerable valiant Christians down through the ages have been that God's presence is most clearly discerned in times that are the most turbulent. Are there many who would dispute that these times in which we live are troubling and frightening? My hope is that in this short book of theology, readers will indeed find good news of encouragement—a Christian theology for turbulent times.

The Augsburg Books series to which this book contributes is entitled Exploring Christian Faith. One who is willing to be an explorer is marked by some degree of impatience and restlessness. I seek to write, therefore, a short primer for restless readers who may feel too engaged in active life to pore over larger theological tomes. At the same time, I hope this little book of theology will whet appetites to engage in deeper study. Rather than offering answers to all burning questions, may it provide enough grist to start readers' mind-mills churning in search of broader learning! To aid in that process, questions to provoke further probing are posed at the conclusion of each chapter. While footnotes are intentionally kept to a minimum, the references cited can lead readers thirsty for more to multiple wells of theological wisdom.

As is so often the case for a writer, this book emerges out of the author's own life experiences, needs, and spiritual yearnings. As a Christian pastor, I have been privileged to preach and teach in numerous venues for over three decades. In parish ministry I had marvelous opportunities to engage in formal and informal sessions with adults, youth, and children where we learned from one another about the great themes of the Christian faith. Such teaching and learning moments have continued in other contexts, including in my current calling as a member of the Gettysburg Seminary community.

The opportunity to devote significant portions of time to the project was afforded during a season of a "semi-sabbatical" (chief executives can never get away entirely for long) from my presidential duties at Gettysburg. I express profound gratitude to the seminary's board of directors for granting this leave, and to my colleagues who pitched in and did extra duty in order to make my time away possible. As always, I am most grateful for the students or *theologs* of Gettysburg Seminary, whose response to God's and the church's call never ceases to inspire me.

I am indebted to the countless teachers—beginning in Sunday school and continuing five decades later as I am often afforded opportunity to "sit at the feet" of seminary colleagues and other distinguished theologians—who have shared the faith, including its rich intellectual dimensions. A few are cited in footnotes or references in the body of the text. Particular gratitude is expressed to those who committed time from their busy lives to serve as readers and reviewers of manuscript drafts: Robert Bacher, Shirley Bacher, James Dunlop, Kristin Johnston Largen, and Kathleen Reed. For some selective "field testing" of the book in nearly final form, I am also indebted to the astute lay theologians who are my children and daughter-in-law: Aaron Cooper, Adam Cooper, Macrina Cooper-White, and Melissa Ramirez Cooper. While these consultants' comments and feedback undoubtedly made this a better book, any inaccuracies or errors (or heresies), of course, are solely my responsibility.

As always, the working relationship with the good folks at Augsburg Fortress Publishers has been positive and professional. Special gratitude is expressed to Gloria Bengston, editor of the Exploring Christian Faith series, who, along with Henry French, Susan Johnson, and Marissa Bauck, has been a superb traveling companion in the final stages of the book's journey toward publication; also to Michael West and Beth Lewis, whose ministry of encouragement keeps authors coming back with more ideas and manuscripts.

Finally, as always, I am indebted to my most important conversation- and life-partner, pastoral theologian Pamela Cooper-White, who never suffers theological foolishness lightly.

1

Starting at the Endgame

Eschatology

The end is near.
The end is here.
In the end—God!

IN CHESS THE FINAL moves before one player vanquishes the other with a quiet or boisterous declaration of "Checkmate" are referred to as the "endgame" phase. The game is all but over. Only a few pieces remain on the board. The player about to win is probably aware of her or his favorable position. The opponent may or may not be aware that things are about to conclude unfavorably. When the game finally ends, an astute observer or the involved contestants might "play back" or review the game from its conclusion to the very first moves. Through careful analysis, the ultimate outcome may have been predictable from the game's very early stages. Or surprise strategies by the winner, perhaps coupled with serious mistakes on the part of the loser, may have resulted in an outcome quite different from typical endgame scenarios.

Down through the ages, many thinkers and writers have suggested that a key factor making us human beings different from other creatures is our ability to ponder life's meanings, to recognize our mortality, and to reflect on both our individual and corporate endgame. In stark, simple terms, we know we are going to die. We see others—including beloved friends and family members—come to their final moments and conclude their lives. And we know it will happen to each of us. All of us who have been privileged to serve in pastoral ministry can testify to the anxiety that accompanies grief when a person is dying. No matter how difficult or painful it may become, life is an extraordinarily precious gift—and none of us wants to lose it.

In broader reflection, especially in light of recent alarming scientific predictions of dramatic climate changes here on planet Earth, and in the face of the ongoing threat to civilization by ever-proliferating weapons of mass destruction, we can even contemplate possible scenarios that would mark the endgame for civilized society, and perhaps for the entire human species.

In theology, to speak or write of the endgame, the final things, is to engage in what is called *eschatology*. The word comes from the Greek *ta eskata*, meaning simply "end" or "final things," and *logos* ("word")—so literally, "a word about the last things."

It may appear strange to begin a work of theology by talking about the final things. That may seem like reading first the final chapter of a novel or good detective mystery. Is not such an approach likely to ruin a good story? In many if not most works of systematic theology, the chapter on eschatology comes where it might be expected—at the end of the book. But one might think of the theological enterprise as akin to building a house or skyscraper. Having a clear picture of the end result before beginning construction is the key to a successful final product. So this work of theology will begin at the endgame and work backward from there.

Many psychologists, sociologists, and anthropologists argue that it is the very contemplation of the last things, especially one's personal death, that drives human beings to ponder and be engaged with matters described as religion, faith, spirituality, or theology. While we might speculate endlessly as to whether a human species that was not mortal—where people never died—would be religious at all, it seems to be the case that thinking about death and what might occur thereafter is one primary aspect of what causes us to wonder about God. There may indeed be true atheists who never think or ponder about a supreme being and who are utterly unconcerned about life's end. But most of us appear to hold out hope for *something* beyond the grave and for *Someone* who will welcome and receive us with love into a new realm of existence.

For either the first-time reader of the Bible or one who is studying it again for the umpteenth time, starting at the back of the book is not a bad approach. Seeing how it all comes out in the end can help interpret everything that goes before. A scholar of Holy Scripture is aware that the ordering of books in the Bible is somewhat arbitrary. Nevertheless, the book of Revelation does in some measure presume to convey how the story of God's relationship with all that God created (told in the Bible's first book, Genesis) will conclude.

And how does the story end? In Scripture's final chapter, the Comeback God promises yet one more time, "Surely I am coming soon" (Rev. 22:20).

Christianity's Endgame Launched at Calvary

On the grand chessboard of the cosmos, the game has been going on for a long time. If the best estimates offered by contemporary cosmologists who study the beginnings of the universe are correct, things have been around for several billion years. Anthropologists and paleontologists who study the origin of the human species estimate that our kind has existed for at least a hundred thousand years.

While the student of cosmology and history might conclude that it truly has been "just one thing after another" for eons, proponents of the Christian viewpoint believe that at one precise moment in time, God made the bold move that inaugurated the final endgame. It came precisely at a time when it appeared that God and the forces of good had fallen so far behind that things were all but lost.

On a makeshift crossbeam of two poles or tree branches plunked down with a thud in a dusty hole on a hillside at the Jerusalem dumping ground hung a condemned man convicted of religious blasphemy and political treason. After several anguished hours of suffering, he is reported to have cried out, "It is finished." And also, "My God, my God, why have you forsaken me?" And then he died. His life story was over. "Checkmate," concluded both the civil and religious authorities alike on that stark, somber Friday afternoon.

But early Sunday morning two days later, mysteriously and inexplicably, the tomb where he had been buried was found empty. Some of his followers began haltingly and fearfully to share among each other that they had experienced him alive again. While they (and we) would never fully understand what had occurred, it became clearer and clearer that the ultimate comeback move of all time had been played out by a God who shouted a final cosmic "Checkmate!" against all the forces of oppression, death, and destruction ever unleashed in the universe.

Eschatology: Personal and Communal, Complete and Still Unfulfilled

A German word used widely in theology to convey the broad concept of an overarching worldview is *Weltanschauung*. The way readers of Scripture interpret this final section of the book of Revelation is critical to their respective worldviews. Those who interpret God's final promise to come again soon as primarily individualistic believe that God will come *for me* if I am faithful and firm in trusting. Others among us who firmly believe God's final promise understand it in a broader holistic and communal framework—God promises to come back *to us*, indeed, to restore the whole creation to its original goodness and bring it to some final stage of completion.

From these distinctive interpretations flow differing approaches to what is often called the *mission* of a Christian community. If God's final promise is understood as applying primarily or exclusively to individuals, then the mission becomes that of "saving souls" or "bringing individuals to a saving faith in God (and Jesus)." On the other hand, if the final promise from the Comeback God is understood communally, globally, and inclusively, the mission of individual believers and of faith communities is also to proclaim God's care for all of creation. Such inclusive belief tends to lead its adherents into work for the renewal of creation, care for the environment, the quest for peace among nations, and greater justice for all citizens of the earth.

Rather than forcing an either/or choice between the personal and communal, Christian theologians can adopt a both/and approach, embracing the twofold eschatology set forth in the New Testament. God's final promise, "I am coming soon," is a word for every individual person. The apostle Paul declares this decisively when he speaks of baptism (see more about this in chapter 8), claiming that each one of us has been baptized into the death and resurrection of Jesus (Rom. 6:1-11). Through baptism and the life of faith, each person is promised that the Comeback God is indeed coming back *for me.*[1] But the teachings of Jesus and the theological declarations of Paul likewise give assurances that God is coming back for the sake of the whole creation, which "will be set free from its bondage to decay and will obtain the freedom of the glory of the children of God" (Rom. 8:21).

Another distinction frequently drawn in theology is between eschatological perspectives that are future-focused and those asserting that promised events have already begun to take place. The latter perspective is often referred to as *realized eschatology*—the view that much of the fulfillment foretold in Scripture, particularly in some of Jesus' preaching and teaching, as well as that of his followers—has already begun to be realized in actuality.[2]

To be sure, a fully realized eschatological perspective would come up short for most of us in terms of fulfilling our greatest hopes for both personal and communal ultimate outcomes. "If this is as good as it gets," we might well conclude, "then God isn't as great as I hoped for and expected!" If the current state of affairs—in which millions of children go to bed hungry and hundreds are murdered on city streets or in war on a daily basis—is the best God can do in the end—is this really the God-Star to whom we want to hitch our wagons?

In a number of Jesus' teachings, as recorded by the New Testament gospel writers, and in some of the most challenging and most comforting words written by Paul in his letters to the early churches, a distinction is drawn that we commonly refer to as the *already/not yet* dialectic. (Another key term in theological discourse and literature, *dialectic*, is derived from usage in modern philosophy wherein seemingly contradictory terms or concepts, in combination, may be understood to point together toward a higher truth.)

All four New Testament Gospels convey Jesus' firm conviction that the final reign of God has already broken into human history. In its simplest variation, the message is reported at the beginning of Mark's gospel where Jesus begins his public ministry in Galilee by declaring, "The time is fulfilled, and the kingdom of God has come near [or 'is at hand']" (Mark 1:15). Notice that Jesus did not speak in the future tense, "The time is about to be fulfilled," but simply in the present, "The time *is* fulfilled." Jesus also set forth some key markers of God's in-breaking reign when he quoted the prophet Isaiah in

Luke 4:18. The one upon whom the Spirit of the Lord has fallen in order to usher in God's new reign will bring good news to the poor, proclaim release to the captives and recovery of sight to the blind, and let the oppressed go free.

While continuing to assert the *already-ness* of God's reign with a sense of urgency in his teaching and preaching, Jesus simultaneously maintained an ongoing tension by declaring that all had not yet been fulfilled. "There's more to the story" was the flip side of the message "It's already all been told." "While we're already in the endgame," Jesus seems to say, "God will yet make some surprising moves that you can't even begin to imagine!" In John's gospel, for example, when Jesus knew that his own endgame was near, he said to his disciples, "I still have many things to say to you, but you cannot bear them now" (John 16:12).

This *already/not yet fully* tension, reiterated throughout the New Testament stories about Jesus, is mirrored in the theological reflections of the church's first systematic theologian, the apostle Paul. In Romans, for example, Paul boldly declares that those who profess faith in Jesus Christ are already rescued from eternal death and damnation—finally and fully saved from the consequences of sin and the powers of evil. Employing language that sounds appropriate in a court of law, Paul asserts unequivocally that believers "are *now* justified by [God's] grace as a gift, through the redemption that is in Christ Jesus" (Rom. 3:24, emphasis added). Yet Paul acknowledges that even the already saved baptized believers continue to endure hardship and sufferings, surely falling short of what is hoped for as final fulfillment of God's great promises. While already justified or made right with God, we continue living (and suffering) and are yet to be fully saved. "Much more surely, having been reconciled [to God], *will we be saved* by [Jesus'] life" (Rom. 5:10, emphasis added).

Two highly regarded theologians of the twentieth century, Oscar Cullman and Emil Brunner, both used the analogy of Christ's death and resurrection being akin to D-day in World War II. While defeat of the German army was secured by the landing of the allies in France, it took several months of continuing severe fighting before VE-day, which marked the war's endgame. Brunner wrote:

> Just as the allied troops after D-day . . . knew that the victory was theirs, even when there lay before them long days and even months of fighting; so Christians, since the D-day of Christ, since the great invasion of the kingdom of God into our history has succeeded and the decisive battle had been fought on the cross, knew that victory was theirs, even when there lay before them long years of fighting.[3]

What Does the Promised "Not Yet" Look Like?

One of the marvels of modern technology, a sonogram, enables expectant parents to see a "picture" of their baby before it is born. Yet even as the technology rises to ever-greater sharpness of image, there is no way a mother or father can really grasp and appreciate the sheer beauty of the tiny creature who is about to enter the world. So it is with the anticipated "not yet" fullness of what God promises in biblical metaphorical language like a "new Jerusalem" or the coming reign of God.

Eschatological visions portrayed in the New Testament or in contemporary sermons and writings cannot begin to capture a true portrayal of what we might anticipate when God finally determines to draw all people to God's own self (John 12:32). Our most expansive mental visions of the promised ultimate glory of God undoubtedly will fall far short of what we will experience when "that day" comes. Whether "that day" comes in a cataclysmic future culmination of history, as suggested in the book of Revelation and some gospel passages, or in some form of resurrection completion while time and history continue on indefinitely is unknowable.[4] But the promise of fulfillment and some form of *eternal life* in the presence of God is sure and certain according to the words of Jesus and the declarations of the New Testament authors.

Writing of the anticipated Great Fulfillment he was absolutely certain was still to come, the apostle Paul recognized nevertheless that "now we see in a mirror, dimly" (1 Cor. 13:12). Just as the grainy dim snapshot of a tiny human fetus does not begin to show the beauty of the glorious baby who will soon be born, so our wildest imaginings will be surpassed when ultimately we "see face to face." But while we can catch only the merest glimpses of the foretold and promised "not yet" that awaits us, we can be confident that God has set forth the broad outlines, as seen most particularly in glimpses of eternity afforded the first apostles as they *saw* and experienced the resurrected Jesus. To that future where the risen Christ has gone before us, the Comeback God beckons us, "Come! Have no fear. I have prepared a place for you, and for the whole creation." Rather than spending precious energy speculating about the "when" and "how" of God's bringing the creation to its ultimate fulfillment (which are unknown even to the angels and the "Son"), Christians are encouraged by Jesus to "keep awake" and "keep alert; for you do not know when the time will come" (Mark 13:32-37).

For Further Pondering and Probing

1. In these early years of the twenty-first century, particularly as we face a global energy crisis, irreversible climate changes, and the continuing threat of annihilation by weapons of mass destruction, is it possible to cling to the notion of *realized eschatology*? How can Christians communicate a credible message that God's eternal reign of peace and harmony is already among us? In a time that cries out for human efforts to save the creation, is it wise to hold out promises that God may suddenly swoop in and rescue the cosmos?

2. Many of the divisions in Christianity result from differing convictions about the "already/not yet fully revealed" balance—between those who claim a high degree of certainty based on God's revelations and those who conclude that much of God's will and many of God's ways are yet to be revealed to humankind. What do you deem essential core beliefs (already revealed), and which questions can remain open for further human insight or divine revelation?

2

Back to the Beginning

Creation

There are only two ways to live: you can live as if nothing is a miracle; you can live as if everything is a miracle.

—Albert Einstein

NOW THAT WE HAVE peeked ahead to the end of the story, let us go back to the beginning and think theologically about the creation. The way we view all matters of theology will be shaped by our perspectives on creation and eschatology. Following this chapter will be one with some introductory comments on the impact of *context* on all theological work, as well as the whole concept of *revelation* or how God clues us in about who God is and how God works in the cosmos.

Most if not all religious traditions include oral and/or written descriptions about the origin of all things. For those of us who embrace the Judeo-Christian heritage, the primary source for our thinking about creation is the first book of the Bible, Genesis, the very meaning of which is "beginnings."

It is important at the outset to consider options and make some decisions about the nature of the book of Genesis, which in turn will influence our overall interpretive or *hermeneutical* (from Gk. *hermeneia*, "to interpret") stance regarding the Bible. Is it a book of scientific fact wherein everything is set forth as literally true and factually correct? On this question hinges a basic theological conviction. Some will answer an unqualified "Yes, indeed!" to this primary hermeneutical question. Others who take a broader (some would say more scientific, modern, or liberal) approach to Scripture will say, "No, the writer of Genesis did not set out to write a factual account that will stand the test of modern science; rather, the author(s) of Genesis offers a theological statement about God's intentions in creating all that exists."

Where Christians of differing perspectives can agree theologically is in the very first assertion of Genesis, that in the beginning God created all that exists. In the Apostles' Creed we declare that "God the Father" (or the so-called first person of the Trinity) is indeed "Creator of heaven and earth." However and whenever the launching of the universe and all that has ever existed occurred, God did it.

But *how* did God bring all things into being? While literalists would say, "Just as the Bible says—in six days simply by issuing commands," many of us conclude, "We really don't have a clue about the mechanics of creation, its timeline, or how God chose to do it." The writer of the Gospel of John waxes theological in the first chapter, suggesting poetically, "In the beginning was the Word, and the Word was with God, and the Word was God" (John 1:1). Creation, for this gospel writer, was by means of God's (the Word's) creative word. God spoke things into being, or perhaps better said, *called* things into existence. Christians who see no incompatibility between faith and scientific theories on the origin of the universe might equate God's first *call* with some sort of cosmic "big bang" that started reality as we know it in motion.

As already noted, many of the great divisions within the universal Christian family have resulted from the differing interpretations of the creation stories. "Stories" is purposely plural in recognition that two distinct versions of the creation appear in the first two chapters of Genesis.[1] Raging religious debates of the past century over evolution hinge in part on whether one can accept the possibility that creation did not occur in six literal days as we know them but gradually over eons of time through intertwined and overlapping complex evolutionary cycles of nature. In contrast to fundamentalist or literalistic interpretations, many reputable theologians today conclude that "there is nothing inherently inconsistent in holding both to evolutionary theory and to faith in God the creator. However extensively we may have to revise our previous assumptions about the time span, stages, and processes of God's creative activity, this does not substantively affect the central claim of faith in God the creator."[2]

Creation as Cosmic Calling: Once for All or Ongoing?

Among the points discussed and disputed for centuries has been the question of what God did prior to the creation of the universe, living beings, and humankind. In his *Confessions*, Augustine quoted and disparaged the old joke that before creation, "God was preparing hell for those prying into the subject."[3]

Despite all the discoveries by scientists who probe the origins of the universe, we cannot fathom whether there was some kind of primordial preexisting "stuff" out of which creation as we know it was fashioned. As the book of faith for Jewish and Christian believers, the Hebrew Bible opens by stating that "the earth was a formless void." So whether original creation was "out of nothing" (Lat., *ex nihilo*) or from primordial "stuff" of some variety, "the Spirit of God moved upon the face of the waters" (Gen. 1:1-2 KJV).

Both Genesis and John's gospel declare that the act of creation involved divine saying or calling: "And God said . . ." "[By God's Word (Jesus)] all things were made." God's Word called forth order out of chaos, light from darkness, firmament from formlessness. God's calling power wrested out of nothingness all that is, including living creatures according to their kind or nature. In what both creation accounts point to as the pinnacle of divine creative activity, God decided to leave a calling card in the form of "our image" (Gen. 1:26). Human beings were created, blessed, and encouraged to "be fruitful and multiply" (v. 28).

Another question often asked relative to God's creative activity is whether it all happened "back then, back there" or is an ongoing process. The latter perspective merits another Latin phrase, *creatio continuo*, or "continuing creation." It is the stance adopted by many theologians who reject a perspective known as *deism*, which sees God as the great cosmic designer-engineer who set things in motion but thereafter left the natural world and all that exists on their own.

The deist position seems incompatible with the rest of the stories told in Genesis and throughout the Bible. Rather than a remote inventor-God who fashioned and then cut loose the great cosmic invention, Genesis goes on to speak of "the LORD God walking in the garden at the time of the evening breeze" (3:8). The Comeback Creator there depicted was already coming back in search of the wayward disobedient human ones held hostage by their own dreams and desires to be like God.

As Genesis goes on, God is portrayed as engaged in an ongoing relationship with the creation, especially humans. At a point where a combination of human disobedience and natural forces appeared to threaten obliteration of all life that could not breathe underwater, God called and coached Noah to build an ark and to rescue and preserve "two of every kind . . . to keep them alive with you" (6:19). This so-called *covenant* (pact or agreement) with Noah was followed by other covenants, key among them the one with Abraham whom God promised to make "the ancestor of a multitude of nations" (17:4). In God's ongoing covenanting with or coming back to wayward human beings, we can see what surely are signs of God's continual creative calling.

For many who first approach the Judeo-Christian tradition, this may be perhaps the most surprising aspect of the so-called creation stories in the book of Genesis. Particularly in a culture such as ours in North America, a person with religious impulses likely would expect the great Creator to be overseeing all the marvels of God's handiwork from some posh palatial skybox in the grand stadium of the universe. But it is not so! Rather, in the metaphorical manner of the writer of Genesis, God is portrayed as hanging out in the garden with the created humans and all the other good creatures: "The man and his wife heard the sound of the LORD God as he was walking in the garden in the cool of the day" (3:8 NIV). In other words, right from the start Creator God became Comeback God who kept coming back to mix it up with those brought into being through God's cosmic calling. Most especially has this been the case whenever we humans have gotten ourselves in trouble and appear "down for the count" or on the verge of full and final defeat and death.

According to Genesis, then, apparently the great cosmic Creator does not deign to assume a higher place of prominence, but rather chooses over and over again to hang out among the masses without a Secret Service detail or other means of protection from human folly. Instead of embracing what surely is God's due—a one-up status over the creatures whose very being came from the Creator's hand—the Divine One assumes a lowly one-down position, setting off in search of the beloved human ones rather than summoning us to a high and holy office or celestial courtroom.

Purposeful Movement, Not Random Roaming on the Sea of Eternity

Just as we cannot know what God did before the creation, or how it was all pulled off by the grand genius Creator, so we humans cannot fully comprehend God's purpose in shaping and molding things as we find them. But we can be certain that the creation has a purpose, that in creating God had a divine strategic plan, and that all creatures who have ever lived play some part and are swept up in this ever-forward-marching movement. History is not, as Henry Ford and other cynics have suggested, "just one damn thing after another."

The purposeful nature of creation is revealed through a close and careful reading of the Genesis texts. Following the creation of the human male and female, God said, "See, I have given you every plant . . . and every tree" (Gen. 1:29). That divine "See" is really a "See here now" mini-lecture similar to what a loving parent must on occasion deliver to a child who has temporarily lost her or his way. It is a "See here now" that means that life has purpose and living ones have destiny, and that we and the whole creation matter profoundly.

The great New Testament theologian Paul of Tarsus (commonly known as Saint Paul) recognized the purposeful nature of the creation in one of his own "See here" declarations. God's creation as a cosmic entity is not like our human creations that have a utility period and then are consumed, abandoned, or discarded. Rather, God's creation, while marred by sin, wasting away of its own self-consumption, or being ravaged by irresponsible human actions and ignorance, "itself will be set free from its bondage to decay and will obtain the freedom of the glory of the children of God" (Rom. 8:21).

That the creation itself is purposeful and goal-oriented signifies that surely human history is going somewhere and that each individual life has meaning and purpose. In contrast to the many religious variations of *dualism* (a philosophy that there are two radically separate and different realms, the spiritual or sacred and the physical or secular), Christian creation theology is deeply holistic and incarnational. As we have seen, Yahweh-Creator[4] did not abandon creation once its initial phase was over. God remains an actor in the ongoing life and development of the creation. Not a remote "owner" who watches play unfold via remote transmission, God is rather a "player-coach" enmeshed in the game of life, coaching alongside us, shaping history.

In keeping with a *creatio continuo* perspective, *process theology*[5] suggests that the ultimate goals for creation may remain up for grabs, that even God may still be evolving and is affected by interactions with the universe. Offering an alternative to a high *transcendence* theology (where God is held to be above and beyond the creation), process theology argues for a high degree of *immanence*, God dwelling in creation. If all things created are still "in process," the reasoning goes, is not the Creator also in a state of ongoing metamorphosis? Most process theologians stop short of *pantheism*, the belief that God is so totally incarnate (embedded) in the creation as to be identical with it. Process theology stands in sharp contrast to radical *predestination*, the conviction that God micromanages the universe according to a detailed divine plan designed in advance of the creation, which is being carried out with no deviations or course corrections.

Classical Christian theology holds to a purposeful creation over which God remains in control with a loving, sovereign guiding hand. The catechism of the Anglican (Episcopal) Church, for example, states of creation "that the universe is good" and "that it is the work of a single loving God who creates, sustains, and directs it."[6] In Martin Luther's Large Catechism, the reformer speaks of God's ongoing hands-on intervention in the creation and especially human affairs: "We also confess that God the Father has given us not only all that we have and what we see before our eyes, but also that he daily guards and defends us against every evil and misfortune."[7]

While the Comeback God remains engaged with and in some measure guides and directs the unfolding of the creation, we must not hold overly high expectations of knowing God on the basis of what is seen and experienced in daily life. While Luther's catechisms taught about a God who can be understood, in many other writings and sermons the reformer speaks also of *Deus absconditus*, the "hidden God" who can only be known partially and whose nature should only be spoken of tentatively. God is revealed to some degree in creation (which is, after all, in the divine image), yet God "hides behind" the creation and can be known only through the Word, which is not bound by but rather transcends creation. Karl Barth took this hiddenness a step further in describing God as "wholly Other." In the towering dogmatic work that propelled him to center stage among theologians of the twentieth century, Barth claimed: "And what is clearly seen to be indisputable reality is the invisibility of God. . . . And what does this mean but that we can know nothing of God, that we are not God, that the Lord is to be feared? Herein lies His pre-eminence over all gods; and here is that which marks Him out as God, as Creator and Redeemer."[8]

Such a view of God as "wholly Other" need not lead to despair or a sense of futility. In the final chapter, we will turn to questions of "How then shall we live?" in the face of a creation that at best only partially reveals God's identity, will, and purpose. Christians can take comfort in the struggles to believe and continue believing that marked the lives of many of those we have come to regard as saints. Luther spoke often of his own *Anfectung* or near despair. After Mother Teresa's death in our own century, her correspondence with several "confessors" reveals her fifty-year struggle to catch glimpses of God's presence and to experience divine responses to her fervent prayers.

Humankind: A Special Species

"What are human beings that you are mindful of them, mortals that you care for them?" asks the psalmist in pondering what is often called the central question of *theological anthropology* (Ps. 8:4). "Who are we and what are we like as human beings?" is the anthropologist's (from Gk. *anthropos*, "man") query. As believers, we ask it from a theological perspective: "Who are we in God's eyes?"

Both Genesis narratives point to humankind as being set apart from the rest of creation to fulfill a special calling. The account in Genesis 1, as we have seen, recounts the Creator fashioning humans "in our image, according to our likeness" (1:26). Humans are to have "dominion" over other creatures (more about this later). The newly created woman and man were blessed by God and encouraged to "be fruitful and multiply, and fill the earth" (1:28), always remembering that all the other species and the whole of creation itself are a gift from God (1:29).

A slightly different emphasis occurs in Genesis 2, where testimony regarding humanity's creation includes the assertion of divine inspiration—literally God's breathing into man and woman the very breath of life (2:7). Among the privileges afforded the humans was that of naming all the other creatures (2:20), thereby taking on a special stewardship responsibility for those named, as does a parent in the awesome responsibility of "giving name" to a child. We are not designed for solo existence but are destined for communion with counterparts: "It is not good that the man should be alone" (2:18). And our kind was created in two coequal genders, male and female, who may come together as "man and wife" and in so joining become "one flesh" (2:24).

Humanity thus stands in a unique and particular relationship with the divine Creator. We human ones are summoned by the Creator into multivalent callings that include "tending the garden" and embracing our God-given ability to "walk and talk" in relationship with the one who gives us life. As we live together in recognition of our common humanity, our relationships within the global community should reflect the mutuality that theologian Letty Russell describes so richly with the images of friendship and partnership.[9]

As we know deep within our bones, of course, in all of these divinely bestowed privileges and responsibilities we fall short! That this is so is explained by Genesis as resulting from what is commonly referred to as "the fall." Disobeying God's boundary-setting instructions, we are no less tempted and no less guilty than our first forebears in our desire to "be like God" (3:5). Therein is the root of all cosmic evil and all human sinfulness. We are not content to accept our God-given place in the universe. We abuse our privilege of "naming" and soon begin to label others of our own kind as inferior, lazy, stupid, and even unworthy of God's love. Granted a degree of *free will*—the right to make choices and decisions—we inevitably make some bad ones that hurt ourselves and harm others. Genesis describes the results of human error and rebellion as our being punished by suffering, and ultimately expulsion from the good garden of original creation. But in reality we separate ourselves from God by overreaching our human limits and going beyond our boundaries.

Despite our irrepressible sinful human tendencies, the testimony of subsequent biblical scripture is that the "divine spark" of original creation in God's own image is never fully extinguished. A measure of obedience to God's boundary-setting ordering of creation remains possible. While the preponderance of humankind lapsed into divine-status-seeking sinfulness, in the words of the old spiritual, "Noah found grace in the eyes of the Lord." Despite our ever-present tendencies to hunker down in a self-protective posture, humankind maintains the ability, at least in some measure, to be "open to the world." In using this phrase as he set forth a theological anthropology, German theologian Wolfhart Pannenberg reflected on our best human tendencies, which include a never-ending quest for new horizons and expanded possibilities.[10]

The best news of all is that the Comeback God never abandons us human ones to our disobedient rebellion. God keeps reaching across the abyss whereby we humans have distanced ourselves.

Yahweh God, self-revealed in the Hebrew scriptures, made promises (covenants) over and over and chose to do "a new thing" in order to draw humanity back into close relationship (Isa. 43:19). While never without backsliding, the human ones hearkened to God's call and responded with renewed obedience. Abraham and Sarah said yes when God called them to go out on a journey with no clear end in sight. Moses accepted the call to liberate his oppressed people from their bondage in Egypt. The prophets of Israel stayed in close relationship with Yahweh as God laid upon them the burden of risking their lives as truth-tellers to the disobedient and despotic ruling power brokers of their time. And when the time arrived in all its fullness for God's final endgame moves, the undimmed *imago Dei* (image of God) in humankind enabled the Spirit to move in and get through with the gospel. The great twentieth-century Roman Catholic theologian Karl Rahner wrote of humanity's capacity to receive and respond to the good news of Jesus Christ. The human, says Rahner, "is a Christ-centered being . . . [who] possesses an ontic and spiritual-personal capacity for communicating with Jesus Christ . . . [who points us] in the direction of God."[11]

Called to Be Creation's Conserver-Stewards

In the first creation story, it is reported that after each act of calling something new into being, God stood back, reviewed the completed work, and concluded, "That's really good!" The created universe gave and gives the Creator great pleasure. As has been noted, upon the conclusion of the original creation, whenever and however that might have occurred, God called upon the humans to tend and nurture the creation. Animals were brought to the first humans to be named, to be respected and cherished. Likewise to be cherished, tended, and stewarded is the entire creation, including the natural environment (described in Genesis 2 as God's beloved lush Garden of Eden).

While all living things require basic sustenance, and many creatures are physically sustained by consuming other life forms, it is hard to imagine that God's intention for creation squares with the consumptive lifestyles of us who live today in the so-called first world. In so many ways and so many places, the original goodness of the creation has been eroded and damaged by human overconsumption, greed, and shortsighted failure to engage in good stewardship practices.

There is truth to the accusation that some of the most exploitive consumptive gluttony has occurred at the hands of Bible believers who misinterpret the meaning of God's command to "have dominion" (Gen. 1:26) over the other creatures. The word *dominion* relates to the Latin word for God (*Dominus*). But if we are to be Godlike in our relationship with the rest of the creation, it is only in the sense that we are to have the same profound love and respect for it as does the divine Creator. We must always remember, as Martin Luther taught in his explanation to the first article of the Apostles' Creed, "I believe that God created me and *all* that exists." We are created ones along with all the other creatures.

Recognizing that all of creation is God's beloved handiwork, to be carefully tended, Christian theologians increasingly have moved among others at the forefront of efforts to promote better environmental stewardship. In 1983 the Sixth Assembly of the World Council of Churches (WCC), meeting in Vancouver, launched an emphasis on "Justice, Peace, and the Integrity of Creation." JPIC, as it came to be called, recognized the importance of joining together concern for all of God's creatures and for the well-being of creation itself. In 1990 the WCC sponsored a World Convocation in Seoul, Republic of Korea, "to engage member churches in a conciliar process of mutual commitment to justice, peace and the integrity of creation." A set of faith-based affirmations was approved by the convocation. Among them were the following:

1. We affirm that all forms of human power and authority are subject to God and accountable to people. This means the right of people to full participation. In Christ, God decisively revealed the meaning of power as compassionate love that prevails over the forces of death.
2. We affirm the full meaning of God's peace. We are called to seek every possible means of establishing justice, achieving peace, and solving conflicts by active nonviolence.
3. We affirm that the world, as God's handiwork, has its own inherent integrity; that land, waters, air, forests, mountains, and all creatures, including humanity, are "good" in God's sight. The integrity of creation has a social aspect, which we recognize as peace with justice, and an ecological aspect, which we recognize in the self-renewing, sustainable character of natural ecosystems.

Bundling Beloved Creation in a Big Receiving Blanket

Many an expectant mother has spent long hours during gestation knitting in anticipation of heading home from the hospital with her newborn bundle of joy wrapped in a soft, warm *receiving* blanket. That image of receiving a beloved, fragile, tender newborn could well serve all of us in search of a faithful posture toward and right relationship with God's great and beautiful yet exposed and vulnerable creation. The strands woven into such a cosmic receiving blanket include a hearty yet not legalistic environmentalism and concrete conservation measures; the quest for healthier lifestyles that both help preserve our bodies and minimize the use of nonrenewable resources and higher animal life forms; and untiring efforts to systematically dismantle and do away with all life- and planet-threatening instruments and weapons, especially nuclear and other armaments capable of mass destructive power.

Just as a newborn baby is wholly dependent on its parents and other caregivers, so God's beautiful creation depends on our long-term loving nurture. And just as parents find great joy in the new inhabitant of their household, albeit often fleetingly amid the demands of constant caretaking, so we can *enjoy* a newfound relationship of mutual interdependence with the creation. We cannot live apart from the daily bread and blessings bestowed on us by the richness of this good earth and its surrounding atmosphere. And the creation cannot continue to live on and bestow its blessings apart from an ever-growing stewardship exercised by its human inhabitants.

In a sermon that became so well-known that an entire book was published bearing its title, theologian Joseph Sittler proclaimed the urgency of approaching "the care of the earth" from a posture of spiritual *enjoyment*, not crass consumerist *usage*. Sittler recognized what every person afflicted with alcoholism or another addiction knows so well: *using* a substance almost inevitably proceeds to abuse. The challenge in our necessary consumption of the creation is to enjoy in moderation, not use and abuse in excess. "Abuse is use without grace," preached Sittler; "it is always a failure in the counterpoint of use and enjoyment."[12]

Since Sittler preached his prescient sermon nearly a half century ago, the call to care for and steward God's good creation has taken on added urgency. What a few scientists back in the mid-1960s (regarded by many as alarmist radicals) hinted at is now a widely accepted fact—our planet Earth's very continuing inhabitability by humans and other creatures is in jeopardy. Our energy-consumptive lifestyle has gone beyond the perils of pollution. We may be inexorably approaching the point of no return as the phenomenon called "global warming" accelerates at an alarming pace. In recent years a growing number of theologians have heard nature's cries for heightened attention and have recognized that the care of creation is not just a matter of human survival but of divine concern.

Contrasting a creation-centered theology, which pays attention to ecology and planet-sustaining economics, with the "neoclassical" stance, whereby Christians concern themselves only with human survival and "dominion" over all other species, Sallie McFague calls for swift and sweeping attitudinal change. The neoclassical model, she asserts, "sees human beings on the planet as similar to a corporation or syndicate, a collection of individuals drawn together to benefit its members by optimal use of natural resources." A new ecological economics, by contrast, "sees the planet more as an organism or a community, which survives and prospers through the interdependence of all its parts, human and nonhuman."[13]

If we can muster the courage to join with others who are committed to enjoy and not abuse the creation, knitting together a giant global receiving blanket in which to bundle and bear every newborn burst of creation-caring, then surely Creator God's voice once more will be heard echoing throughout the cosmos, "This is good; this is really, really good!"

For Further Pondering and Probing

1. A contemporary controversy swirls around what should be taught in public schools about the beginnings of the universe and human beings—the theory of evolution or some variation of "creationism" or "intelligent design" that posits or allows for a divine Creator. What are your thoughts on these often-divisive debates?
2. Is not the conviction that "prayer changes things" based on a view that God is indeed affected by human pleas? If one believes that creation was purely past divine activity ("back then, back there"), does it make any sense to pray?

3

Theology as Talking Back to God

Context and Revelation

God is not a God of the emotions, but the God of Truth.

—Dietrich Bonhoeffer[1]

NOW THAT WE HAVE begun "doing" a bit of theology, pondering both where the creation might end up and how it all began, it is time for a brief diversion into matters frequently referred to as *context* and *means of revelation.* In reflecting on context, we note that a theologian's vantage point or "social location" will inevitably shape how she or he goes about the task of theological reflection. In exploring means of revelation, we will delve into various ways by which it is thought that God reveals to us God's nature, will, and ways with the world.

As children we may have been cautioned by parents, teachers, and other adults against "talking back" to our superiors. While it appears less so today than in previous generations, millions of us in our younger years heard and often heeded the old adage that "children are to be seen and not heard."

When the triune God determined, "Let us make humankind in our image" (Gen. 1:26), and then proceeded to invite the human ones to speak and name the other creatures (Gen. 2:19-20), it was made evident that God truly desires and enjoys a "talk-back species." The process and practice of doing theology, no less than offering prayer and praise in worship, are a primary means of talking back to God. In speaking and writing words (Gk. *logoi*) about God (Gk. *theos*), we deploy God-given fledgling faith in search of deeper faith and more profound understanding of the great mysteries of God's nature,[2] will, and calling for individuals, communities, and the whole cosmos. At the same time, theology is work in service to the church. Theologizing lays a foundation for teaching, for passing along with integrity the faith handed down to us from the apostles entrusted by God with first shaping the Christian gospel message.

Context: God Always Comes Back in a Specific Time and Place

A word introduced previously—*dialectic*—may best describe the nature of God's self-revelation and God's own very being as portrayed in the Bible. On the one hand, there is an unchanging timelessness to the divine nature and being, suggested in the New Testament claim that "Jesus Christ is the same yesterday and today and forever" (Hebrews 13:8). On the other hand, however, God (Yahweh), as described in many Old Testament passages, is often depicted as changing God's mind or "repenting," as in the altering of plans to totally demolish an entire community (see, for example, Jonah 3:10

where God abandons plans to destroy the city of Nineveh). The prophet Isaiah declares that God is "doing a new thing" (Isa. 43:19). Multiple biblical references to prayer—including the sustained prayer life of Jesus—likewise suggest that God's responses to human suffering and desires can be influenced by the pleas and petitions of those who pray humbly "in spirit and truth" (John 4:23) and praise "with the spirit . . . with the mind also" (1 Cor. 14:15).

Living in this dialectic tension that embraces both God's eternal, unchanging, essential nature and God's ever-evolving response to cosmic context and human situations, we recognize that the theological enterprise is likewise held in a delicate balance. It is always Christian theology's task to tell the same message as told by the first followers of Jesus who proclaimed the core gospel message: "He is risen and he saves!" That is to say, our task is ever and always to pass on to those new to the faith in each generation the *apostolic faith*—the same core beliefs first formulated by the apostles in response to Jesus' life and teachings and their experience of his resurrection. Simultaneously, the challenge remains to make the message relevant, intelligible, and meaningful in the current context—for ourselves and those who find themselves in very different social locations from our own.

Another word with Greek origins, *exegesis* ("to draw out"), is frequently used in describing the task of careful and close reading and study of biblical texts in order to discover their true meaning. Theologians who recognize the contextual nature of God's self-revelation—who understand that the Comeback God always "comes back" to us in a specific time and particular situation—likewise understand the importance of exegeting the current context. Thus, the theologian lives in each dialectical moment, asking both, "What was God's message and meaning at some point in the past?" and "What is God up to now in our time and place, among this community in which we are gathered, including for me as one among billions of persons created in the image of God?"

As new understandings and greater wisdom concerning the world and human nature become available, for example, through knowledge gained in scientific endeavors, understandings of God's will and intention may indeed change over time. Multiple examples readily come to mind: the change in many churches regarding ordained service by women; the switch from upholding slavery and other racist practices on the basis of a few biblical passages; and the abandonment of rigid adherence to a whole host of archaic and culture-bound laws, regulations, and dietary restrictions set forth in Leviticus and other parts of the Old Testament.

When individual believers, local faith communities, or entire national and global church bodies change positions on a given issue, does this mean that those in earlier generations were necessarily wrong in their stances? In some cases, especially where the domination and oppression of individuals and entire groups of people resulted, unequivocally yes. But in other ways—for example, when new insights gained through scientific discoveries or the unearthing of additional original manuscripts for a portion of scripture are involved—it may be unnecessary and unhelpful to regard our forebears as wrongheaded or hard-hearted. Many of us grew up in an era before seat belts and child restraint devices were routinely available and installed in motor vehicles. Does that mean our parents and other drivers who transported us were neglectful and remiss? No, indeed; however, given the technology available presently, any of us who have others' lives entrusted into our hands today as we hit the roadways would be irresponsible in failing to insist, "Fasten your seat belts."

For Christians, the incarnation (the enfleshment) of God in the Bethlehem-born baby named Jesus stands at the heart of the Good News, or gospel. The second article of the Apostles' Creed declares his incarnation: he was "born of the virgin Mary." Like all newborns, he came into the world at a specific time, lived in a particular cultural milieu, was raised by real human parents, and was formed as a person within a thoroughly Jewish community and society under Roman occupation and domination. As is true for every human, Jesus' own social locale shaped his worldview, his *Weltanschauung*. His teaching and preaching were highly contextual. The stories or parables he told employed images and examples, which those who traveled with him or came out to hear him readily understood, and with which those living in first-century agrarian and urban environments could easily identify.

The social location in which we citizens of the early twenty-first century find ourselves is radically different from the context in which Jesus, his followers, and subsequent generations of Christians lived, taught, and sought to be faithful disciples. Within our world today, God's beloved human creatures live within a multitude of radically different cultural, economic, and social contexts. The world looks very different to a little girl born in extreme poverty, eking out a meager existence by street begging, than it does to the CEO of a multinational corporation living in a posh mansion and breezing daily around the world in the corporate jet.

A growing recognition of the critical importance of recognizing, exegeting, and understanding the implications of context and social location has led to a much broader concept of "theology" itself. Over the course of the past half century, growing numbers of theologians have come to embrace the notion that there is not one monolithic *theology*, but rather a multiplicity of *theologies*, even within a single faith tradition. While previous generations of Christian theologians believed that each world religion had its own corpus or body of theology, we who engage in theological work today recognize that within Christianity there are a host of strains and quite different historical and contemporary interpretive traditions.

To be sure, even within mainstream Christianity there have always been significant or nuanced theological differences, especially since the Reformation of the sixteenth century when the broad "catholic" tradition divided into Roman Catholic and Protestant trajectories. But beginning with liberation theology flowing out of Latin America in the late 1960s, a host of distinct theologies has been ever-expanding and flourishing. Theologians who take context seriously have spawned a marvelous body of Christian theologies that hold sway under such banners as feminist, black, womanist, *Minjung* (Korean heritage), Native American, Asian, and *mujerista* (Latin American women's perspective).[3]

Each of these new theological traditions includes a critique of classical theology authored and taught predominantly by those who are sometimes referred to as DWMs (dead white males). While committed to convey, out of their personal life journeys and those of fellow travelers, the same message as that spoken by Jesus' first followers (that is, the grand "apostolic faith"), especially on the unmarked pathways trodden by the poor and oppressed who live far beyond the main thoroughfares of modern life, these newer theologians seek to contextualize the gospel so that it might become truly Good News to their communities and to us all. In other words, it is important to recognize that black theology is not just for African Americans nor is feminist theology only for women. Those of us who find ourselves in privileged positions (and surely I must include myself as a white, middle-class, highly educated American male clergyman) may have the most to learn from our sisters and brothers who speak, write, and theologize from what is often described as "the underside of history."[4]

The Current Context: *Postmodernism*

Historians, philosophers, sociologists, and theologians who seek to understand the grand story of the human journey tend to use broad, sweeping generalizations or categories to describe entire historical eras. College courses and even entire departments often are described with appellations like *primeval*, *ancient*, *medieval*, and *modern*. We speak of broad historical eras as primitive, prescientific, industrial, and technological.

Over the past three decades or so, beginning with origins in the work of some French philosophers, the current historical, social, philosophical, scientific, and political scene has been described by many thinkers as *postmodern*. One is unlikely to attend a conference on topics of sociology, philosophy, literature, theology, or psychology today without soon hearing from one speaker or another the assertion that we live in the postmodern age. What does this mean?

Postmodernism is described by comparison and contrast to previous historical eras. In the "ancient world," before modern science, worldviews were shaped in small communities often isolated from one another. Those with access to the limited body of knowledge contained in books or taught by scholars at academies or fledgling universities were few in number. Interestingly enough, the "queen of the sciences" in the premodern world was theology, with theologians and clergy often among the best-educated and most highly regarded persons in a community. Conclusions about the nature of the world were based on limited perspectives without access to the tools of science we simply take for granted. Observations limited to the naked eye reasonably concluded that the earth is flat and at the center of the universe with the sun and all the stars revolving around it. Absent any evidence of microscopic bacteria and other forces at work in all organisms, the causes of disease were quite respectably chalked up to mysterious unseen causal forces called demons. Much that could not be explained was attributed to divine or demonic intervention. Devoid of any reason not to do so, most texts—like the Bible—were taken literally.

Then came the scientific age, which ushered in what was broadly regarded as "the modern world." This era, in which the light of science began to shine into many dark corners, has also been referred to as the Age of Enlightenment. The rapid expansion of knowledge, created with the aid of an ever-growing array of scientific instruments and tools, revolutionized human understandings of the world and broader cosmos. Astronomy, medicine, biology, physics, chemistry, and all the other sciences contributed to ever-expanding knowledge that provides explanations for phenomena previously attributed to divine or demonic activity. Some scientific discoveries and the theories advanced to explain them have had profound impact on theology and communities of faith. The theory of evolution, for example, set the religious world back on its heels and forced many biblical scholars to rethink their interpretations of what the first Genesis creation story really means in speaking of the seven "days" of creation. Perhaps the writer of Genesis can be understood to describe prolonged evolutionary eras rather than literal twenty-four-hour periods.

As advances in physical science were occurring in the modern era, so too new approaches emerged in the social sciences and fields of knowledge commonly referred to as "the liberal arts." New frameworks for reading and interpreting literature in all fields (often described with a word introduced previously—*hermeneutics*) began to be applied by modernizing biblical scholars in what became known as "higher criticism." Using various forms of literary, textual, and contextual analyses, professional scholars, as well as those often called "the laity," began to read the Bible with an eye toward questioning long-held assumptions. In the recognition that—like all other authors—the biblical writers crafted their messages within their own social locations and contextual realities, many Christians began to question whether new conclusions to age-old vexing questions might be possible. In the modern milieu, for example, apparent biblical endorsements for the oppressive practice of slavery and the suppression of women were reexamined. Individual believers, congregations and religious communities, and entire church bodies changed their positions, with some becoming champions in the abolitionist movement and embracing the gifts of women for service in the ordained ministry.

The impact of modernism in shaping newly emerging worldviews has been enormous. Among its many influences has been the forging of new understandings of and approaches to authority. In the premodern era, when theology was queen of the sciences, the declaration of a priest or preacher on most matters was widely regarded as the conclusive "last word" beyond questioning. In the modern era, the faithful have wisely become much more prone to respond, "Now wait just a moment, Reverend! Let's discuss this in light of my experiences and my professional scientific knowledge, which far exceed your own." This modern eagerness to question long-held assumptions and willingness to revise previous stances gave rise to even greater tensions and fragmentations within faith traditions. Both in local congregations and broader church bodies (which in North America are known as denominations), controversies sparked by the influence of modernism fueled conflicts that often soon became church-dividing. We continue to see such effects in the rifts and divisions caused by contemporary debates over a host of issues related to human sexuality, abortion, the ethical appropriateness of stem cell research, and the like.

While in a number of respects the strains and stanzas of the great modernism symphony continue ringing in our ears, many thinkers, writers, and speakers in recent decades have been contending that yet another threshold has been crossed in the history of humanity.[5] A key "composer" contributing to this new symphony on the cosmic stage has been yet another scientific development of the twentieth-century—quantum physics. Albert Einstein's theory of relativity and accompanying breakthroughs, which led to the nuclear age, forced fundamental rethinking of the nature of matter, energy, and the ways of the universe. Whereas earlier Newtonian physics and more sophisticated understandings that evolved in the modern age argued for a highly predictable universe (becoming ever more so with each new scientific discovery), the theories of quantum mechanics point toward a more fluid and less predictable cosmos, where more things are up for grabs, and random forces beyond control can cause surprising outcomes.

To use a simplistic analogy, the modern era led us to believe that given the right kind of measuring instrument, anything and everything can be measured, categorized, and understood with a high degree of precision. Such scientific theories as Werner Heisenberg's "uncertainty principle" point to a radically opposing perspective that says that any scientific investigation changes the very things it is exploring. A scientist conducting any kind of experiment is like a person measuring an ice cube with a hot ruler! Things can never be finally and fully pinned down. The postmodernist appreciates and applauds, to a degree the ancient Greek philosopher never could, Heraclitus's assertions that "all things are in flux" and "you can never step into the same river twice."

Theology as Taking Off in Several Directions

While modernism challenged many certainties accepted without question in premodern times, it did not lead to such fundamental skepticism as has been manifested in much of postmodern philosophical reflection. To be sure, modernists raised questions in many arenas about the way things really happened. Long-held assumptions and conclusions were questioned. But that there remains an overarching "grand narrative" to describe the structure and development of the universe was not thrown in doubt to the extent now experienced in the postmodern era. Stuart Sim, in his editor's introduction to *The Routledge Companion to Postmodernism*, offers a succinct synopsis of this current era in the history of intellectual reflection:

> In a general sense, postmodernism is to be regarded as a rejection of many, if not most, of the cultural certainties on which life in the West has been structured over the last

> couple of centuries. It has called into question our commitment to cultural "progress" (that economies must continue to grow, the quality of life to keep improving indefinitely, etc.), as well as the political systems that have underpinned this belief. . . . Postmodernists are invariably critical of universalizing theories ("grand narratives" or "metanarratives" as they have been dubbed by the philosopher Jean-François Lyotard), as well as being anti-authoritarian in their outlook. To move from the modern to the postmodern is to embrace skepticism about what our culture stands for and strives for.[6]

In such a context, theological reflection and the faith communities in which it takes place have experienced during the past half century what theologian Paul Tillich described in the title of one of his best-known sermons, "the shaking of the foundations."[7] Whereas in past generations a pastor or Sunday school teacher could make certain assumptions about commonly held basic values and worldviews on the part of her or his hearers, those of us committed to "contend for the faith that was once for all entrusted to the saints" (Jude 3) have no such solid foundations on which to build.

At stake in the debates swirling amid the turbulent waters of postmodernism is the fundamental question posed to the accused Jesus by his one-man judge and jury, Pontius Pilate: "What is truth?" (John 18:38). Or stated more radically, many seekers deeply influenced by postmodernism may ask, "Is there finally any overarching truth at all?" From a variety of directions, they will hear a definite "No, at least when it comes to the big questions of meaning, purpose, and universally embraced core values and ethical principles." For the radical postmodernist, all of reality is a constantly changing ice cube, and in our attempts to comprehend it, we bring only hot rulers. In approaching texts, values, systems, institutions, and entire bodies of knowledge, the postmodernist's task, therefore, is to *deconstruct*[8] long-held assumptions and conclusions. Literary critics and other interpreters approach all texts, including the Bible, with a "hermeneutics of suspicion" that in essence suggests questioning everything, especially that which has long been held to be true. Rather than valuing vast experience and credentials overly much, deconstruct them lest they exert coercive domination and impede your ability to discern your own truth.

At the time of this book's writing, we are engaged as a nation in our every-four-year cycle of preparing to elect the president of the United States. In a *New York Times Magazine* opinion piece, one astute observer noted that the current field of candidates is perhaps the least experienced ever in terms of offering credentials of significant long-term service in major state or federal executive offices. He concludes:

> American politics can never be viewed in isolation from the rest of society, and something deeper has been happening out there. The emergence of the Internet age has been accompanied, in general, by a steady devaluing of expertise. A generation ago, you went to the doctor to find out about the pain in your knee; now you go to WebMD, diagnose it yourself and tell him what medicines you want. . . . Suddenly, experience is downright suspect—it's the barrier that so-called professionals use to wall themselves off from everyone else.[9]

Christian theology has often been framed as setting forth the grand, sweeping story of God's saving activity in relationship to both individuals and the world. This is described by a German word, *Heilsgeschichte*, or "history of salvation." From a postmodern perspective, any such grand narrative that asserts overarching paradigms and sweeping generalizations about a loving, yearning God who keeps coming back to save that which God created must be questioned, critiqued, and deconstructed through an unremitting hermeneutics of suspicion.

In such a context, a theologian who practices in the world of belief and the unseen would appear to have no firm ground whatsoever on which to stand. If no texts—including the Bible, Koran, and other sacred scriptures of the world's great long-standing religions—are privileged texts whose meanings take precedence over other writings, to what do we point as the source of truth? In the postmodern world, traditional authority figures—the highly educated, teachers including clergy—have no special standing; their assertions and declarations are no more valid and carry no more weight than the opinions of anyone else. Perhaps the best way to describe the place of the theologian in the postmodern world, then, is with the phrase once used by a doctoral student to capture the innovative approach of the American Lutheran theologian Joseph Sittler: "With both feet firmly planted in midair, he takes off in several directions!"[10]

The World in Which We Live: Global, Diverse, and Pluralistic

If *postmodern* is one major descriptor of our world in these early years of the twenty-first century, two other key ones are *global* and *pluralistic.* While the world has always been a global village as seen through God's eyes, we humans have never before been as conscious of our fellow villagers as we find ourselves now. The impact of rapid transportation modes and instantaneous worldwide communication media has forever altered our perceptions. Commercial exchanges across national borders used to be a rarity; now they are routine and daily. The rapid spread of the English language enables ever-expanding direct communication apart from the need to await tedious translation. As a result of the emergence of "world wars" in the twentieth century, the dislocation of millions of refugees, coupled with voluntary migration, resulted in a worldwide intermingling of peoples not previously experienced in history.

Diversity and pluralism mark today's planet-wide community. Increasingly, they also become markers of individual nations. We who live in North America need no reminder of growing diversity as we simply look around ourselves in the waiting areas of any major airport. And yet, as we know so well, harmony is often a missing marker. The very richness of God's good creation often threatens, and we humans become self-protective against those whose difference calls into question some of our cherished values and habits. Many who have lived securely and comfortably, shielded from the poverty and suffering endured by billions of our fellow earth-dwellers, have been forced to see reality as it confronts them daily on their big-screen televisions. Those content in being "on top of the world" economically, socially, and in terms of wielding power now are threatened by the conclusion of Thomas L. Friedman's book that "the world is flat."[11] Access to information has been leveled in extraordinary measure by the explosive growth of the Internet and mobile phone industry. Often our children and grandchildren learn from, interact with, and get to know (virtually) playmates across an ocean before they meet those who live just down the street.

Nowhere do the results of globalization and growing pluralism become more personal (and for many in a threatening way) than in the area of our most cherished beliefs or religion. In generations past, large segments of the population in most locales tended to live among "our own kind" when it came to religion. To be sure, in the days my grammar school granted "religious release time" once a month, we divided three ways and trekked off to the local Lutheran, Presbyterian, and Roman Catholic churches in our little farm village. But in most U.S. communities today, were such a practice reinstated, students would also head toward the local synagogue, mosque, or Buddhist temple, and of course growing numbers would stay behind in the classroom as a result of adhering to no organized religious tradition. The presumption that in any locale a majority of residents hold similar values, practice common customs, and are generally shaped by a broad homogeneous "culture" simply can no longer be made. In the postmodern age, we all live increasingly in daily commerce with a richly diverse, pluralistic global community.

Revelation: How and Where Does God Disrobe for Us?

Now that we have considered the importance of paying attention to context in doing theology and recognized our placement amid the twenty-first-century global community of ever-expanding diversity, this chapter will conclude with some brief comments on the important topic of *revelation*. When all seems up for grabs, amid the constantly shifting borders and boundaries of communities and nations, with our feet firmly planted in midair, where are we to look for the face (or maybe at best some traces) of God?

The image of God disrobing may be a rather jolting one for many readers. But the literal meaning of revelation is an unveiling, or the showing of that which has been hidden, covered, unseen, and unknown. Questions related to revelation are as old as theology itself. They ask, "Where do we look for God, and how do we know when we are catching glimpses of the Divine?" "How do we sort through all the competing claims made about God to know what God is really like and what God's will is for us and for the universe?" "Can we ever fully know God? If not, why does God stay somewhat hidden from us?"

A theologian's understandings about revelation will be shaped by several variables, including her or his own social location, context, theological method, and worldview. A radical postmodernist response to the questions of revelation might well be, "We can know virtually nothing with certainty about any god if there is one; each person can only speculate and draw personal conclusions. There is no Truth; there are only multiple and individual truths." A fundamentalist perspective on revelation would go something like, "All we have to do is read the Bible, where God is fully and clearly revealed, and where God's plan for the universe and every person is crystal clear." The theologian whose primary method is scientific is likely to say, "We can learn most about God through giving careful attention to empirical discoveries, paying attention to how God ordered the universe." A theologian who leans in a heavily devotional or mystical direction may suggest, "We can best know God through prayer and contemplation, both solitary and communal."

Many theologians find it helpful to distinguish between *general* and *special* revelation. These thinkers propose that much about God can be known to everyone, religious and nonreligious alike. Much about the nature of the Creator can be discovered by observing and pondering the creation. Fundamental revelations about God's intent for society and divine expectations for moral conduct are implanted in everyone's conscience, whether atheist or fervent faith-adherent. The "natural law" written into the warp and woof of the universe is available for all human beings to discern and follow. Such revelation(s) falls in the broad category of general revelation.[12] Special revelation, according to this framework, is explicitly religious in nature and comes to us through channels that open to those who give ourselves over to a life of faith. It is given through sacred scriptures, accessed through personal prayer and communal worship, transmitted generation to generation through church teachings (often called doctrine), mediated in a particular way and with special intensity through sacraments or "means of grace."

For the broad spectrum of Christianity that regards itself as "mainstream" (neither conservative-fundamentalist nor radical-revolutionary), revelation is understood as a blend of general and special. Much about God is known to all in creation and in myriad observations of human interactions and the inherent goodness that can be witnessed all around us in daily life. But the one true God can be distinguished from all the lesser pretend gods only by careful attention to sacred texts, experience seen through the lenses of faith as passed down through generations by Christian tradition, and reasonable pondering and prayer within a worshipping community that corrects individual misperceptions and encourages continuing discovery of the fullness of God's love. This threefold nature of revelation is summarized within world Anglicanism and other communions in shorthand: God is known through reading *scripture*, by exercising our best human *reason*, and in paying close attention to the teachings of the Christian *tradition*.[13]

Even within mainstream Christianity, however, there is perennial debate about the whole matter of human agency in revelation. Can we do anything to learn more about who God is and what the Almighty One desires for us? Or are we passive recipients totally dependent on God's self-revelation? In Martin Luther's Small Catechism, the latter view is maintained in his explanation to the third article of the Apostles' Creed: "I believe that by my own understanding or strength I cannot believe in Jesus Christ my Lord or come to him, but instead the Holy Spirit has called me through the gospel, enlightened me with his gifts, made me holy and kept me in the true faith, just as he calls, gathers, enlightens, and makes holy the whole Christian church on earth and keeps it with Jesus Christ in the one common, true faith."[14] Others, including many Lutherans, believe that while salvation and justification are pure gifts totally dependent on God's grace, we can open ourselves to divine revelation through spiritual practices, careful attention to Scripture, and frequent communal discernment that trusts the Spirit's leading.[15]

While the degree to which God can be known is also pondered by theologians, most seem to conclude that we will always live in the already/not yet dialectic described in chapter 1. In this life we can experience God's presence and know God's nature and will to some degree ("in a mirror dimly"), but God's more complete unveiling always eludes us this side of the *parousia*—the final and full in-breaking presence of God (also described as Jesus' "second coming"). Whether or not God will ever be fully revealed to us in the larger life of God beyond resurrection is unknowable. But as it is in our relationships with other human beings, so with God it seems like the more we know, the more we recognize the "wholly otherness" or altogether unknowability of God.[16] No matter how much revealed, God remains *Deus absconditus*—the "hidden God." An Old Testament passage commonly cited in this discussion is Exodus 33, where Moses prays to God, "Show me your glory," and God's response is an unequivocal, "You cannot see my face; for no one shall see me and live." "At best," says the ethereal Divine One who often remains elusive, "I'll give you some occasional glimpses of my backside!"

While God's self-revelation to humankind will always remain partial and incomplete, God chose at a particular moment ("in the fullness of time") to exercise the most complete epiphany (or "manifestation") in the person of Jesus of Nazareth. In the incarnation, the great cosmic Creator, the one clothed in all the glory of universe upon universe, in fact *disrobed* and was born naked through the usual messy, bloody, painful process. And at the opposite end of Jesus' life, God's own self hung disrobed on a cross in the garbage dump on the outskirts of the city of Jerusalem. Whoever or whatever else God may be, the God Christians worship and adore, the one to whom we entrust our lives, future, and fate, is a God of the manger and God of the cross. Whatever else we may say about the God whom we recognize and revere, this God came back human and embraced our lot all the way to its conclusion in death. And this same Comeback God promises to keep coming back—each day in the midst of our joys and troubles, and in some more ultimate manner at time's end.

For Further Pondering and Probing

1. Ponder your own "social location" and how it shapes your worldview on a whole host of matters. Imagine a person of similar age and the same gender, but in a radically different

context and lifestyle. How would your imaginary doppelgänger perhaps have quite different views about God (the triune God) and the way God is active in the world?

2. Do you consider yourself a "postmodern person" or one who is more traditional in the ways you view the world? Where do you come down on the matter of "truth" as being objective, hard and fast, once and always the same, or highly subjective, fluid, and changing?
3. Where does God most clearly self-reveal for you and your faith community? When truths taught by the Bible appear to contradict modern science or your own experience, how do you reconcile these diverse perspectives? How do you cope with God's ongoing "hiddenness"?

4

The Comeback God's Playbook

Scripture

The Bible is the manger in which the Christ child lies.

—Martin Luther

IN CHAPTER 3 WE began to delve into the nature of God's self-revelation, noting that the primary window into divine nature and being for Christians is the Bible. Before going on to ponder other major theological themes or doctrines, we will explore more fully the nature and interpretation of the Bible, or "Holy Scripture" as it is often called.

While not an exhaustive cookbook with proven recipes to face every life situation, the Bible may be thought of as God's playbook with broad outlines for how to carry out faithful personal and corporate discipleship. Or using another metaphor, the Bible may be imagined as a choreography design book to broadly structure and set in motion the faith community's dance with the Divine. But first and foremost, the Bible is the "good book" that conveys the good news of God's love for the world and for each of us! That is to say, while it is a guidebook for us as players in the divine drama and game of life, its most important guidance is this: Always remember the Author (God) and God's great gift of life, salvation, and shalom.

Our English word *Bible* comes from Latin and Greek origins, wherein *biblos* meant simply "book." The Bible is, of course, really a book of books, a compendium of sixty-six discrete written scriptures authored by dozens of writers over a period of a thousand years or more.[1] Its largest portion is the Hebrew Bible (also commonly called the Old Testament)—scriptures that evolved out of faith communities in which various strains of Near Eastern peoples chronicled their experiences with the God Yahweh. In its grand sweep, the Hebrew Bible sets forth imaginative perspectives on the prehistoric creation, tells the story of the formation of a "people of God" through the deliverance of a nomadic band from slavery in Egypt (the exodus), and then traces the history of this faith community (Israel) in its subsequent walk with God.

The second major section of the Bible, the New Testament or Christian scriptures, includes four Gospels that relate some of the life story and teachings of Jesus of Nazareth, record and interpret the events surrounding his horrible death, celebrate the remarkable news of his resurrection, and then offer glimpses into the life and thought of the early Christian community. The New Testament also includes a record of the early church's formation and fledgling efforts to cope with overwhelming challenges in carrying out Jesus' missionary mandate (the book of Acts); a collection of letters by the apostle Paul and other writers, which address pressing issues and offer encouragement to early Christian communities; and a selection of apocalyptic literature, the book of Revelation.

Even a cursory examination of the Bible reveals to the novice reader that it contains a broad array of different kinds of literature. There are brief and extended stories, long and rather tedious lists of names, detailed descriptions of certain vehicles (for example, Noah's ark) and edifices (the temple), long prophetic discourses, songs of praise (for example, many of the psalms, Mary's Magnificat), both brief and extensive letters or epistles, and many other types of material. Beginning in the nineteenth century, the recognition of the value of carefully discerning the type of literature being studied in a given section of the Bible led to broad fields of study that are summarized in shorthand as *literary* and *form criticism*.[2] ("Criticism" in this sense does not mean tearing down or finding fault, but simply in-depth and analytical examination of texts using all the tools available to a careful reader of scripture.)

In addition to noting the various types of literature included in the Bible, modern approaches to scriptural study recognize the complexity of its authorship. For example, while historically the first five books of the Old Testament (known as the Pentateuch, "five books," or Torah, "books of the Law") were attributed to a common author, Moses, a careful examination of the literature suggests that many writers' hands were at work in recording and transmitting to later generations the rich and diverse material. Likewise, several generations of New Testament scholars have concluded that not all the epistles attributed to Paul were likely the fruits of his own prolific pen but were in fact written by others and attributed to the great apostle.

Contrary to popular impressions, thus, the Bible was not dropped from heaven as a completed compendium of all scripture worthy of consideration by faithful God-fearing folk! Prolonged discussions, debates, and sometimes extended council meetings were needed before the Christian church would come to consensus on what materials ought to be included in the official *canon* (from Gk. *canonikos*, meaning "rule" or that which is circumscribed by a fence).

Likewise, both Hebrew and Christian faith communities recognize that the various parts of Scripture ought not to be afforded equal value or weight in terms of attention and importance for guiding our lives and mission today. Martin Luther, for instance, "made fundamental distinctions between the books by applying *a christological canon of interpretation*: the gospel of free grace and justification through faith alone."[3] Luther spoke of the book of James as being a "straw epistle" and went so far as to say that it, as well as Revelation, should perhaps be excluded from the Bible because it failed to meet the Christological criterion.

The twentieth-century biblical theologian Ernst Käsemann commented extensively on the Christian community's need to discern the "canon within the canon," focusing our greatest attention on those portions of Scripture that point to Christ.[4] The never-ending process of determining which relatively few portions of Scripture will be read in public services of worship (these are called *pericopes*, from Greek words meaning "seen from a common perspective") reveals this reality that faith communities must make reasoned decisions regarding the relative importance and value of various parts of the Bible.

Scriptural Interpretation: Church Forming and Church Storming

Textual interpretation in any field of literature is often described in shorthand as *hermeneutics*. The particular hermeneutical approach of a Christian community will shape its approach to the Bible and its teachings and lifestyle. While all Christian communions recognize the centrality of Scripture and generally describe it one way or another as being the "source and norm for proclamation, faith and life,"[5] the way in which it is interpreted has led to the major and minor divisions within the one, holy, catholic, and apostolic church. Additionally, the *place* of Scripture vis-à-vis other influential factors is likewise of enormous influence in the life of a community and broader communion. The Reformation-heritage churches tend to follow Martin Luther's insistence on *sola scriptura*, a stance claiming that nothing else comes anywhere close to the Bible in informing the church's beliefs and actions. In tension with that view is a broad strain within Christianity (perhaps reflected most acutely in the Roman Catholic and Orthodox churches) that, while tipping toward Scripture as the highest authority, regards *tradition* (the continually accumulating body of knowledge and wisdom acquired as holy history moves along) as also indispensable. In keeping with its self-description as *via media* or "middle way," the Anglican/Episcopal communion points to three primary sources of revelation and authority: Scripture, the church's tradition, and human reason.[6]

While there are manifold variations of and nuanced approaches to scriptural interpretation, they may be summarized in two broad categories: fundamentalist and historical-critical. These two streams flow from some basic assumptions about the nature of divine inspiration. A *fundamentalist* approach to the Bible insists on its inerrancy, or infallibility in all regards, believing that God dictated the development of the Holy Scriptures to the extent of almost whispering every word in the ears of the original authors. In contrast, the *historical-critical* method sees the Bible, while a unique source of divine revelation, as also in continuity with all other human-generated literature. According to this hermeneutical approach, God was surely involved in inspiring the many writers who recorded the experiences and insights of God's people down through history; but those writers were bound within their own contextual realities and prescientific worldviews, which led to some characterizations of reality that do not stand up in the light of contemporary knowledge. A classic example of the two approaches is evident in how the Genesis creation stories are interpreted. Biblical fundamentalists insist upon a literal reading that the earth and all its inhabitants were created in six twenty-four-hour days. More modernist interpreters conclude that the "days" of creation can be conceived of as long historical eons, and therefore biblical creation theology need not be in contrast with scientific evolutionary theories.

Interpreted from a historical-critical perspective, the Bible is recognized as containing a broad spectrum of theologies addressed to specific faith communities in particular contexts and at unique periods of time. A key task in biblical interpretation, therefore, is the attempt to "read behind the texts" and discover the life-situation (*sitz im leben* in German) or peculiar circumstances being experienced by those to whom a text was originally addressed. Such a hermeneutical approach will, for example, recognize that the seemingly bizarre imagery in the book of Revelation is really "code word" by which early Christian communities facing persecution—their *sitz im leben*—received repeatedly the promise and proclamation: "God has not forgotten you in your distress; the Comeback God will come back for you and for all who are faithful!"

This modern historical-critical process of "reading behind the texts" entered a new era in the twentieth century through the work of biblical theologians like Rudolf Bultmann. The great German scholar's exegetical commentaries and particularly his book, *Kerygma and Myth*,[7] sent shock waves through the academic world and churches. According to Bultmann, the Scriptures—like all significant texts of antiquity—need to be demythologized or stripped of all the accrued layers of interpretation painted over their plain and simple original meanings. Bultmann's and other scholars' use of technical words like *myth* have often been misunderstood to suggest that those who approach scriptures in this way regard the Bible as pure fable or fiction devoid of any historical basis.

Partly in reaction to the broad historical-critical movement, another "school" of New Testament biblical theologians has developed over the past century. Beginning a century ago with the pioneering work of Albert Schweitzer (*The Quest for the Historical Jesus*, first published in 1906) and others, these scholars have engaged in efforts to rescue "the true Jesus" portrait from its biblical and cultural distortions. Their reasoning goes like this: If so much of the biblical witness has been shaped and reshaped by its *redactors* ("editors" who have taken kernels of original material and embellished, rearranged, and reinterpreted so as to bolster their particular points of view), then surely the stories about and sayings attributed to Jesus have also "changed the picture" so much that the Jesus who appears in the New Testament likely bears small resemblance to the itinerant rabbi who wandered about Galilee in the first century. A current conclave of scholars that convenes periodically calls itself the Jesus Seminar. As these scholars sift through the Gospels, they actually cast votes by means of dropping colored beads into a box, offering their opinions on whether a New Testament verse or passage was likely uttered by Jesus.

Over the past several decades, the study of Scripture has branched out in several directions from the basic "trunk" of the historical-critical approach. Claudia Tikkun Setzer offers a succinct summary of the work of some of today's prominent New Testament theologians and the various pictures they paint of Jesus:

> Current scholars draw upon many disciplines, borrowing anthropological and sociological methods. For example, [John Dominic] Crossan relies on some of the insights of anthropology to illumine agrarian peasant Mediterranean society. Richard Horsley and others use sociological data to understand Jesus as a radical political figure responding to economic and political persecution.
>
> A number of different portraits of Jesus have emerged. Marcus Borg portrays Jesus as a religious ecstatic, a teacher of wisdom and a social prophet, focused on the present. "Jesus' relation to the spirit was the source of everything that he was," Borg claims. Burton Mack describes Jesus as a Jewish cynic, a popular sage who shocked people into understanding with his sharp and disturbing sayings. Like

> Borg, he sees Jesus as focused on the present state of the world, a dispenser of timeless truths. Crossan pictures him as a preacher of radical egalitarianism, addressing a peasant society suffering in political and economic straits, offering a message of healing: "You are healed healers, so take the kingdom to others, for I am not its patron and you are not its brokers. It is, was, and always will be available to any who want it."
>
> An essential point of Crossan and others' thought is that Jesus was not preaching himself and his own aggrandizement, but preaching God's kingdom. E. P. Sanders agrees but shifts the emphasis to the future. He sees Jesus as an eschatological prophet, a figure who prepared the people for the coming of God's kingdom, which God would bring in the future. John Meier combines present and future, suggesting Jesus is an eschatological teacher who sees God's kingly rule as already present, but not yet complete, in his ministry. God's plan to establish His rule over His people has yet to come to fullness.[8]

In one way or another, all of the historic and contemporary theologies trace their roots to and bolster their arguments with Scripture. The so-called theology of liberation, for example, orbits around the exodus story in which an enslaved band of Hebrews was led forth from slavery into freedom by the mighty liberating hand of God. So also, say the liberationists, will God's contemporary impoverished and economically and/or politically enslaved faithful find their liberation in the gospel and its incarnation in actions and movements that are revolutionary, that is, that turn society in radically new directions. Various manifestations of feminist theology take with utmost seriousness texts that reveal the often countercultural attitudes and actions whereby women in the Bible were taken seriously, were called to leadership (including as first witnesses to and proclaimers of the resurrection of Jesus), and served as full partners with men in fulfilling the mission of God.

Liberationists, feminists, proponents of black theology, and others who plow new ground in biblical interpretation have described their interpretive approach as of necessity a *hermeneutic of suspicion*. Since the preponderance of biblical interpretation down through the ages has been by men (and in recent centuries Northern European–heritage white males), traditional renderings of texts (even Bible translations) must be viewed with a suspicious eye, keeping open the possibility that long-accepted meanings are distorted or biased. Another word now frequently used to describe such approaches to biblical and theological rethinking is *deconstruction*. Over the centuries, broad conclusions about "what the Bible says" have constructed an imposing theological edifice (recall the introduction of *Weltanschauung* or worldview in chapter 1). Layer upon layer of assigned meaning(s) have been built up that now must be systematically and unwaveringly "deconstructed" in order to get down to the original core messages biblical authors sought to convey. Such thorough textual deconstruction requires finely honed skills that include the ability to read texts in their original languages, recognizing that the very act of translation is itself interpretation (for a translator will be influenced by his or her own worldview in transporting a text from one tongue to another).

The results of such rereading of texts in the light of modern science, postmodern philosophy, and liberationist/deconstructive perspectives have often been "church storming," that is, painful and even traumatic for local faith communities and broader ecclesial communions. At the same time, such "liberative" rereadings of Scripture have opened the church's doors to many who previously felt themselves excluded and unable to receive its good news. The deconstruction of theological foundations that supported slavery, apartheid, and other manifestations of racism caused seismic shakings in congregations, denominations, and global communions in the second half of the twentieth century.[9] It also came as stunning good news to millions of God's children who had been marginalized and oppressed in both the church and larger society. Likewise, deconstructing textual interpretations long used to uphold a ban on ordaining women shook the foundations in many churches and continues to be church-dividing in some measure.[10] And it has brought to the church's clerical ranks thousands upon thousands of gifted women whose liberated energy has been transformative in many settings.

Currently, among the most divisive issues in the largest number of churches is the topic of human sexuality, and in particular, homosexuality. While it is difficult to argue that the Bible offers texts in either testament that affirm intimate sexual relations between members of the same gender, many see the necessity of reassessing traditional conclusions that condemn homosexual orientation and expressions thereof.[11] Such biblical interpreters, often described disparagingly as "revisionist," are persuaded that both Old and New Testament authors, including Paul, may have been unaware of the reality that some persons have innate homosexual orientation and do not choose their affection for persons of the same gender.

Complex matters of Christian ethics like this are unlikely to be settled in the near future. As has always been the case, Christians reading the same Bible texts come to differing conclusions about their meanings. We may take comfort that we are saved by God's grace and not by a perfect "right reading" of Scripture. This does not relieve us of responsibility to prayerfully embrace the Bible as the authoritative source and norm for faith and life.

The Multivalent Nature of Scripture: A Prayer Book Too

As many who have attended a theological seminary recognize, there is a danger in approaching the academic study of Scripture, particularly from a historical-critical point of view. Over time, a Bible student can begin to regard it as just one more book of great literature to be perused and analyzed. There are perhaps similarities here to a couple who fall in love, get married, and soon begin to lose the romance amid the details of daily life together. The husband who regards his wife primarily as cook and coworker will soon discover the luster has worn off their romantic relationship; so too for the wife who sees her spouse more as handyman and child-care sharer than friend and lover. "Keeping the romance alive" with Scripture by recognizing its multivalent nature is a key for people of faith who would look to their book of faith for inspiration as well as education, to uplift as much as to inform.

Accordingly, careful and sustained devotional use of Scripture should be practiced often. Some believers find it most practical and profitable to engage in frequent corporate devotions. The long tradition kept alive by cloistered monks and nuns of "praying the hours" centers around scriptural readings, particularly chanting and reciting together the Psalter. For others, private devotions, which include portions of Scripture—perhaps one's first reading of the morning before the daily newspaper—keep the romance alive with the Bible as personal prayer book, as well as playbook offering guidance for life.

In addition to keeping abreast of new books, articles, and Internet resources in the ever-expanding fields of theology, a theologian needs to stay close to the Scriptures, scrutinizing each new wind of theology in the Bible's brilliant light to see if it meets Martin Luther's key hermeneutical test—*was Christum treibet* ("that which proclaims Christ").

For Further Pondering and Probing

1. In chapter 3 we discovered how postmodernism is often construed to suggest that there are no absolute truths. By

contrast, biblical *fundamentalism* asserts that absolute truth can be found through a literal reading of the Bible. What is your personal response to Pilate's question "What is truth?" (John 18:38). To what extent is the Bible the "source and norm" in your faith and life?

2. Ponder some conflicts in your congregation or other church arenas. To what extent have they been ignited or fueled by differing interpretations of Scripture? What interpretive (hermeneutical) principles are in play among your friends, family members, and others in your circles?

5

Three Times Our God

Trinity

So you're once, twice, three times a lady. . . .
And I love you![1]

THUS CROON THE COMMODORES over and over in an enduring popular song written in the late 1970s by Lionel Richie. Our Christian confession—in worship as well as in the work of theology—is similar: "So you're once, twice, three times our God. . . . And we love you!" Unlike the lover who bespoke his adoration of a singular beloved one, the object of our songs of praise is a three-person unity, the God we also call the Trinity.

There is probably no more difficult and challenging task for theologians than to think, speak, or write about the doctrine of the Trinity. So central to theology and the church is it, however, that in liturgical traditions a Sunday of the church year is set aside to ruminate on its meaning. Even so, despite preachers' best efforts to explain, it is doubtful that most devout believers go home on Trinity Sunday with a clear grasp of the meaning and importance of this doctrine for faith and churchly existence.

We probably have all had the experience of attempting to describe something and ending up exasperated—"I just can't find the words!" It's like that in every human attempt to explain the Trinity. Nevertheless, so crucial is this matter to theology that we must make the effort, despite the fact that, like all theologians down through twenty centuries, in the attempt we will end up "busting our heads"![2]

A question on some college or seminary introductory theology course exams is "Who or what is God?" While it may not be articulated with quite these same words, a question being asked by millions of people around the world is "To which of the many gods worshipped by my contemporaries should I pay allegiance?" While these crucial questions can be approached from any number of perspectives, an adequate Christian response must assert the inherent triuneness of the God revealed most fully in Jesus Christ. Whatever or whomever else God is, God is the Triune One, named in the New Testament "Father, Son, and Holy Spirit" (Matt. 28:19).

Robert Jenson sums up the importance of *talking Trinity* on the part of the church: "Trinitarian discourse is Christianity's effort to identify the God who has claimed us."[3] When we are asked, "Which god do you worship and stake your life and eternal destiny upon?" we Christians answer, "Why, the triune one, of course!" Duane Larson likewise declares that "the Trinity is the root of the Christian confession. . . . The doctrine was and is the primal explanation of how a transcendent God so other-than-the-world could yet create and relate to this world."[4]

When we say, "Father, Son, and Holy Spirit," we attempt to capture in human words the inexpressible essential nature of the Divine.

Recognizing that the triune God created us in God's own image, and not the other way around, we must be careful not to "make God look just like us." This perennial human tendency is called *anthropomorphizing*, that is, conceiving of the Divine in human terms (or reducing the great transcendent Trinity to our meager frame of reference). Conceiving of God the Father as a male human parent, for example, fails to express the true nature of the one who declares, "My thoughts are not your thoughts, nor are your ways my ways" (Isa. 55:8). We can never fully comprehend the entire scope and full significance of the Triune One.

Nevertheless, while triune Father-Son-Spirit always remains elusive and always somewhat beyond our grasp, the Divine One is a real living eternal being who is *personal* among us and *relational* with us. Some of the church's great hymnody points to this *all-encompassing* trinitarian nature and being. God is described cosmically as the one "who made the earth and heaven,"[5] "who stretched the spangled heavens,"[6] "whose farm is all creation."[7] And God is also described in intimate personal terms as "my Lord, my strength,"[8] "God of the sparrow,"[9] and "my faithful God."[10]

God is made known or revealed to us as three persons, yet God remains "one in being" (Nicene Creed). The three persons are coequal—they are "of one being" and "one substance." All are present in all divine actions, from creation onward. As noted in chapter 2, the Gospel of John declares that "in the beginning was the Word [Jesus], and the Word was with God, and the Word was God." While much in the tradition, including the creeds, suggests a differentiation among the three persons of the Trinity in terms of functions (Father as Creator, Son as Redeemer, and Holy Spirit as Sanctifier), coequality of the three persons (or "identities" of God, as proposed by Jenson to capture the Greek *hypostasis* and avoid popular misconceptions of polytheism or belief in many gods) means that all three are involved in creation, redemption, and sanctification.[11]

A particular challenge in describing the Trinity is to avoid what is often described as *modalism*. This theological error suggests that God merely appears to be trinitarian by self-revealing in three distinct modes or media. Modalists teach that God is not really three persons but only appears to be by wearing distinct costumes or disguises. Over against modalism stands the creedal declaration that God is inherently three-personed ("Father, Son, and Holy Spirit") yet unitary ("one God"). It is not merely that God self-reveals by showing us three persons, but that God exists eternally and always in a three-personed holy community-of-one. Before the creation of the universe, there was holy conversation in the three-personed divine essence. Before the separation of light and darkness, God "danced the night away" in a divine triangle of harmonious creative energy. From the get-go, our God is inherently and irremediably *relational*, not just externally in connecting with all the beloved creatures made by God's hand, but internally. Within God's very self there is deep and abiding relational essence. God cannot be other than relational.

The distinction drawn in the preceding paragraph is often described by two words: *economic* and *immanent*. A narrower economic trinitarian view asserts that we cannot know for certain whether God is intrinsically and inherently threefold; but we discern from God's way of interacting with the world that God has chosen and established a threefold "economy" of household management (from Gk. *oikos*, "house," + *nemein*, "to manage") by which to create, redeem, and embrace humankind. A comprehensive trinitarian theology, however, rejects this limited view and argues that, to be fully the God we know and praise, the Divine One is inherently threefold—that is, that relational trinitarianism is *immanent* or indwelling in the very nature of God. Another way of grasping the distinction is that God's trinitarian nature is not just a convenient theory or explanation of how we observe the Divine One at work in the history of salvation, but God is Trinity apart from any human observation or pondering. In other words, God was Trinity before humans began to ponder the matter at all.

Is the New Testament Trinity the Same God as Yahweh of the Old Testament?

As people of faith begin to struggle with the concept of the Trinity, often the question is asked, "So did God change and become trinitarian when Jesus was sent by God to save us?" This question builds from recognition that there is no explicit reference to a three-person Divine One in the Hebrew Bible (commonly referred to by Christians as the "Old Testament"). One of the features of Yahwism, which differentiated the God of Israel from most other religions of the time, was its monotheistic nature. "Our God is one God," declared the Hebrew people.

Surprising to many readers, there is also scant reference to the Trinity in the New Testament. The threefold divine name Father, Son, and Holy Spirit is declared by Jesus only in his final command to go and baptize (Matt. 28:19). Paul made reference to the threefold God in his benedictory conclusion to 2 Corinthians: "The grace of the Lord Jesus Christ, the love of God, and the communion of the Holy Spirit be with all of you" (13:13).

It was probably the very scarcity of explicit trinitarian reference in Holy Scripture that caused the early church to give so much attention to establishing a definitive stance. Had things been spelled out more clearly in the Bible, the first four centuries might have been much easier for our Christian forebears. Endless debates over matters related to the Trinity finally came to culmination in 325 when the Council of Nicea was convened to set forth a churchwide declaration of the apostolic faith. The very brief document that ultimately ensued, which we call the Nicene Creed, is arguably the single most significant declaration of the church beyond the Bible. It established the coequality of the three persons of the Trinity.

Building on the grand declaration of the Word's (Jesus') presence at creation set forth in John 1, the Council of Nicea claimed unequivocally that "through him all things were made." It established firmly that Jesus is "not made" (or created) by God, but "begotten"—that is, of the one same divine essence; and that the Holy Spirit similarly "proceeds from (that is, is not created by) the Father and the Son." The bishops gathered at Nicea further made the connection between Yahweh, the one true God who authored creation, and the same divine trinitarian presence at work in salvation and sanctification or "Spirit life-giving." The Holy Spirit is "the Lord, the giver of life; with the Father and the Son the Spirit is worshipped and glorified."

God's self-revelation as the Triune One arrived at its fullness in the events of Jesus' incarnation, crucifixion, and resurrection/ascension. But this God-incarnate-in-Jesus is no new, improved God beyond the one made known in the Hebrew Bible. As the German theologian Jürgen Moltmann recognized, Scripture and the church's great ecumenical creeds establish firmly that "it was *Yahweh*, the God of Abraham, of Isaac and of Jacob, the God of the promise, who raised Jesus from the dead. Who the God is who is revealed in and by Jesus, emerges only in his [*sic*] difference from and identity with, the God of the Old Testament."[12]

Is "Father, Son, Holy Spirit" the Only Appropriate Name for God?

The question "Is 'Father, Son, Holy Spirit' the only appropriate name for God?" has caused intense and often rather heated debate among theologians over the past thirty years or so. Some theologians who take seriously their contemporary contexts and personal realities have critiqued use of the traditional threefold name of God. Many feminists in particular find problematic the male-gendered reference to Father and Son. Sociological and psychological have revealed that the most commonly used threefold divine name creates mental images for many if not most people of a God who resembles their own or someone else's father or grandfather, and of a Savior who looks a lot like a favorite brother or son. Elizabeth Johnson observes, "Clear and distinct Trinitarian terms give the impression that theology has God sighted through a high-powered telescope, with descriptions of the interactions between three persons intended to be taken in some literal sense." This tendency to accept the "uncritically held assumption that maleness is of the essence of the triune God . . . has the sociological effect of casting men into the role of God while women stand as dependent and sinful humanity."[13]

Alternatives proposed and commonly in use—Creator, Redeemer, and Sanctifier probably being the most employed in public worship invocations—are critiqued as bordering on if not crossing over into modalism. And unlike Father, Son, and Holy Spirit, alternative trifold appellations for the Divine One are not sanctioned by Scripture.

The broad consensus within the universal church at present, reflected in the approved liturgies or worship services of most denominations and communions, is that Father, Son, Holy Spirit remains what might be considered the "legal name of God."[14] But how often must it be employed by a community that would remain true to the apostolic faith? We probably all know individuals whose legal name is seldom used—perhaps only in signing a marriage license, mortgage, or other legally binding contractual document. While the debates will long continue, the broad ecumenical consensus reflected in pastoral teachings, as well as in official ecclesiastical policies, is that the "legal name of God"—Father, Son, and Holy Spirit—is used at baptism.[15] Lest the centrality of the Trinity for Christian faith become eroded, the threefold divine name should also be used regularly in public worship. At the same time, given the very valid concern that careless overuse of male God-language is a stumbling block for many would-be believers, gender-inclusive references to God should also liberally mark our prayers, proclamation, and publications.[16]

Beyond Doctrine: Trinity as Divine Dance Partner

A potential pitfall for all theologians—lay as well as professionals who make their living engaging in God-talk—is that we become so focused on correct doctrine, precise statements, and avoidance of errors that the sheer delight of being in fellowship and communion with the triune God is lost. The very essence of trinitarian theology is to affirm God's *relationality*—the Creator's deeply passionate love for us creatures, the Savior's profound pathos in identifying with the highs and lows of our humanity, and the Spirit's unceasing infusion of dynamic power into individuals and communities.

If they are not artists themselves, theologians do well to rely on artistic renderings of theological concepts in order that the very loveliness of God not be lost amid a plethora of written and spoken words. Images like Rublev's classic iconographic portrayal of the Trinity[17] can convey far better than theological tomes the dynamic relationality within the three-person God.

Pastoral theologian Pamela Cooper-White creates an imaginative word picture in her description of the Trinity as "a spacious room—even a matrix/womb, in which multiple metaphors can flourish, honoring simultaneously the relationality and the multiplicity of God."[18] This image of divine hospitality-in-Trinity can be lived out in the celebration of the Eucharist, where people are welcomed at the Trinity's table.

In the rural Midwestern congregation of my childhood, every Sunday service began with the choir marching down the aisle singing the great nineteenth-century hymn "Holy, Holy, Holy." As a teenager I joined the choir and soon came to know this classic song of praise by heart as week after week we invoked the name of "God in three persons, blessed Trinity." The recent advent of a new worship book in my denomination has introduced a delightful twenty-first-century hymn, which draws singers into new imagery of a dancing Trinity:

Come, join the dance of Trinity, before all worlds begun—
The interweaving of the Three, the Father, Spirit, Son.
The universe of space and time did not arise by chance,
But as the Three, in love and hope, made room within their dance.

Come, see the face of Trinity, newborn in Bethlehem;
Then bloodied by a crown of thorns outside Jerusalem.
The dance of Trinity is meant for human flesh and bone;
When fear confines the dance in death, God rolls away the stone.

Come, speak aloud of Trinity, as wind and tongues of flame
Set people free at Pentecost to tell the Savior's name.
We know the yoke of sin and death, our necks have worn it smooth;
Go tell the world of weight and woe that we are free to move!

Within the dance of Trinity, before all worlds begun,
We sing the praises of the Three, the Father, Spirit, Son.
Let voices rise and interweave, by love and hope set free,
To shape in song this joy, this life: the dance of Trinity.[19]

As we embrace the gift of gospel bestowed by God, it dawns on us that we too are invited into the "dance of Trinity." The divine inherent trinitarian relationality cannot be contained within God's own self but freely "spills over" and washes upon us in never-ceasing waves of grace. Such intimate personal communion with the cosmic Holy One is possible, however, only as God "comes down" and dances with us in our chaotic, messy human arena. In other words, only an *incarnate* (from Latin, meaning "to make flesh") God can draw us into the divine dance of Trinity. We turn to God's incarnation in Jesus and the nature and activity of the divine Savior-Son in the following chapter.

For Further Pondering and Probing

1. In the third century, a huge theological controversy was created when the Alexandrian presbyter Arius began teaching that Jesus was not coequal with God the Father and the Spirit. While Jesus was considered divine by Arians, he was a "lesser partner" created by the Father. Have you encountered modern versions of Arianism or other teachings by Christians who doubt or dispute classic trinitarianism? Why do what appear to be fine distinctions matter so much?
2. Where do you come down in the debates surrounding the importance of using more inclusive language for God, while still upholding the triune name? What have you found to be comfortable imagery for God that remains true to biblical teaching and the catholic faith?

6

God Is Always One-Down among Us

Christology and Soteriology

For I decided to know nothing among you except Jesus Christ, and him crucified.

—1 CORINTHIANS 2:2

THIS CHAPTER ON THE person and work of Jesus Christ begins with a short little word that is not a favorite term for most of us: *sin*. Though we might wish to avoid it, Christians sooner or later must acknowledge sin's reality and presence in ourselves and the world around us. At its core, sin or estrangement from God, self, and one's neighbor results from our ever-present human tendency to practice one-upmanship. While most of us at least grasp intellectually Paul's advice "not to think of yourself more highly than you ought" (Rom.

12:3), we cannot help but posture to secure and maintain a "better than others" status.

According to the Genesis creation story, the desire for a higher-than-human status lies at the root of all sin and waywardness. The temptation to be "like God, knowing good and evil" (3:5) was found irresistible by our first forebears. And the enmity between human beings was manifest in Adam's futile effort to present himself as blameless, or at least better than his companion: "The woman whom you gave to be with me, she gave me fruit from the tree, and I ate" (3:12).

Throughout the history of the divine journey with a particular community—the Hebrew people—the Comeback God kept seeking ways to bring individuals and an entire people back into right relationship. That is to say, God was continually searching for means to save and restore Israel and the whole creation. God's multiple comeback strategies, chronicled in the Old Testament, are commonly called *covenants*. A covenant is simply a promise or declaration of intent. "I will save and bless you" was God's covenantal promise issued over and over again to the people of Israel. God covenanted with Noah after the great flood never again to destroy the whole creation. To Abraham and Sarah, God promised a multitude of descendants. To Moses, and to Israel as a people, God promised deliverance from bondage in Egypt and a journey to a promised land. In the persons and proclamations of the prophets, God continued coming back over and over again in efforts to restore, to rescue, and to save a people from their wayward foibles and repeated unfaithfulness. In spite of God's continual comebacks, the irresistible temptations toward one-upmanship prevailed in luring human beings into oppressive behaviors and attitudes, violence and destruction of one another and of the good creation.

Following centuries or perhaps eons of deploying one after another comeback strategy, God decided to try a new way. "When the fullness of time had come, God sent his Son, born of a woman" (Gal.

4:4), to save us from the results of all our deadly one-up endeavors. This sent-by-God-one, Jesus, was and is God's "final answer" for the future of the cosmos. But contrary to long-held messianic expectations of a Great One-Up who would rule and lord it over humankind and all creation, in the sent-one Jesus, the Comeback God came as a servant, one-down among us.

Teachings about and doctrine concerning Jesus Christ fall within an area of theology commonly called *Christology* (literally, "words about Christ"). *Soteriology* (from Gk. *Soter*, "savior") concerns the saving work of Jesus. Ruminating about who Jesus is and the significance of his life, teachings, and saving actions draws us into these two dimensions of theology.

A still widely used symbol for Christianity, the fish, dates back to the earliest days of the Christian movement when it was used to mark gathering places for the fledgling faith communities. In addition to perhaps reminding the early apostles of Jesus' many associations with fishing activity—including the final resurrection appearance story in John's gospel—the Greek word for "fish" constituted an acronym, *ICTHUS*, which signaled to knowing insiders, "Jesus Christ, God's Son—the Savior." In its essential shorthand form, this simple phrase constitutes the heart of Christology. Jesus is the incarnate (enfleshed) "second person of the Trinity" called "Son," and this Jesus is the Savior of the whole cosmos. Jesus is God "deep in the flesh" (Luther), and also the one who "is seated at the right hand of the Father" in glory (Nicene Creed).

John the Baptist, who was Jesus' way-preparer, declared in the wilderness that "the kingdom of heaven" was coming near. John went on to make the audacious claim that unlike himself, who baptized merely with water, the coming one would "baptize . . . with the Holy Spirit and fire" (Matt. 3:1-12). In the moment of Jesus' baptism by John in the river Jordan, the voice of God was heard in a grand Christological pronouncement: "You are my Son, the Beloved; with you I am well pleased" (Luke 3:22). Further confirmation of his cosmic significance was signaled by the Spirit's baptismal presence in the form of a dove.

The great Christological question was posed repeatedly by Jesus himself and by his initial followers, as well as by his detractors and opponents. Midway in Matthew's gospel, the imprisoned Baptist reconsidered what he heard at the Jordan and sent a message to Jesus, asking, "Are you the one who is to come, or are we to wait for another?" (Matt. 11:3). Later on his journey, Jesus himself asked his followers, "Who do people say that the Son of Man is?" Then he focused in on his own disciples: "But who do you say that I am?" In response, Simon Peter blurted out the Christological claim that continues to be voiced by Jesus' followers today: "You are the Messiah [Christ], the Son of the living God" (Matt. 16:13-16).

Confronted with Jesus' power over even wind and waves in the story of the storm's quieting, the disciples asked of one another, "Who then is this, that he commands even the winds and the water, and they obey him?" (Luke 8:25). Right up to the end, threatened and paranoid religious and civil authorities were asking, "Who is this one about whom many are making claims that he is King of the Jews or even the Son of God?" Faced with Jesus' dying outcry as he breathed his last, "My God, my God, why have you forsaken me?"—the ultimate expression of being one-down for the sake of the world—a Roman centurion summed up the life of the Crucified One: "Truly this man was God's Son!" (Mark 15:34, 39).

The New Testament Gospels and book of Acts are extended Christological statements. Each seeks to set forth claims about Jesus, both his person and impact. Particularly in John's gospel, a plethora of metaphors is ascribed to Jesus in an attempt to set forth who he was and is for us: Emmanuel ("God with us"), the Lord; Lamb of God; Bread of Life; the Way, Truth, and Life; Living Water; Son of God; Son of Man; True Vine; Good Shepherd.

In Jesus, God "Poured It Out and Poured It On" for Us!

The epistles of the New Testament, each typically addressing burning questions in one or more of the early Christian communities, are compelling Christological statements. Writer of several, Paul was constantly wrestling with the great Christological questions and often combating false interpretations that were beginning to spread like wildfire during the early years of the Christian movement. Prominent among the New Testament Christological statements is the so-called *kenotic* (from Gk. *kenosis*, "pouring out") confession in Philippians 2:5-11:

> *Let the same mind be in you that was in Christ Jesus,*
>
> *who, though he was in the form of God,*
> *did not regard equality with God*
> *as something to be exploited,*
> *but emptied himself [literally, "poured himself out"]*
> *taking the form of a slave,*
> *being born in human likeness.*
> *And being found in human form,*
> *he humbled himself*
> *and became obedient to the point of death—*
> *even death on a cross.*
>
> *Therefore God also highly exalted him*
> *and gave him the name*
> *that is above every name,*
> *so that at the name of Jesus*
> *every knee should bend,*
> *in heaven and on earth and under the earth,*
> *and every tongue should confess*
> *that Jesus Christ is Lord,*
> *to the glory of God the Father.*

This self-emptying or "pouring out" on God's part in the incarnation has been maintained by the church in every age as a response to recurring erroneous Christological formulations, many of which have suggested that Jesus only appeared to be completely human or fully divine.[1] To make understandable the claim that while Jesus became fully human he also remained entirely divine, the doctrine of the two natures of Christ evolved in early Christian teaching. How these two natures—divine and human—interrelate has been posed in the language of philosophy utilizing a Latin phrase, *communicatio idiomatum*, or the intercommunion and inextricably intertwined communication of human flesh and divine spirit. Debates over the two natures persisted after the Nicean Council for more than a century, during which two "schools" (at Alexandria and Antioch) argued priority for the divine and human natures respectively. At the Council of Chalcedon in 451, a declaration was issued to establish the "consubstantial" (Gk. *homoousion*) full presence of both humanity and divinity in Jesus.[2]

A Jesus who was not fully human would remain one-up over us, unable to take on the full measure of human pathos, pain, and peril. And, of course, a messianic figure who was any less than divine would not have brought to bear the salvific powers Jesus displayed in his earthly life and continues to exercise today. In short, as declared the imprisoned German theologian soon to be martyred by the Nazis, Dietrich Bonhoeffer, "The Bible directs man [*sic*] to God's powerlessness and suffering; only the suffering God can help."[3] Only the one who is simultaneously fully God and truly human can be the Savior.

Debates concerning the two natures were not settled once and for all with the pronouncements of Chalcedon, of course. They would resurface a millennium later in the context of the so-called Protestant reformation. Seeking to set forth their clear teachings on the matter, Lutheran Reformers declared in the Augsburg Confession that their teaching is

> that the Word, that is, the son of God, took upon himself human nature in the womb of the blessed Virgin Mary so that there might be two natures, divine and human, inseparably conjoined in the unity of one person, one Christ, truly God and truly a human being, being "born of the Virgin Mary," who truly "suffered, was crucified, died, and was buried" that he might reconcile the Father to us and be a sacrifice not only for original guilt but also for all actual sins of human being.[4]

Soteriology: The Comeback God Makes the Final Moves

As noted in chapter 1 on eschatology, Christian theology does well to begin with and return often to the divine moves of the endgame that have already been played on the cosmic chessboard. Looked at in more depth, God's actions in the events of the crucifixion and resurrection of Jesus constitute the heart of what theologians have long referred to under the broad concept of soteriology.

The impact of Jesus' life, teachings, crucifixion, and resurrection has been described using several classical theological terms: *salvation*, *justification*, *redemption*, and *atonement*. More recently, contemporary theologians have expanded the repertoire of soteriological descriptors with words like *liberating*, *shalom-restoring*, *justice-bringing*, *victory-achieving* (Jesus as *Christus Victor*[5]) and others that are emerging as individuals and faith communities "translate" the gospel so that it becomes meaningful in their own contexts and worldviews.

Thanks especially to the creative and impassioned work of liberation and feminist theologians in recent decades, a great deal of rethinking classical soteriological claims has begun. Noting that "the maleness of Christ as imaged through the centuries has damaged women's self-esteem by relegating us to second-class citizens,"

Lisa Isherwood poses the radical question "Can a male savior save women?"[6] Carter Heyward speaks of the necessity of "pruning away some of the tangle of Christological clutter" that obscures who Jesus is and what he means for us. She speaks of being "more interested in images of Jesus as brother and friend than of Christ as King and Lord."[7] James Cone asks, "What has the gospel of Jesus Christ to do with Black people's struggle for justice in a white racist society?" He concludes that a proper Christological understanding must be grounded in the conviction that "no interpretation of the Christian faith could be valid without an engagement of the issues of justice in the society and the world."[8] Elsa Tamez also emphasizes the importance of Christological probing to determine who Jesus is for the victims of oppressive one-upmanship:

> The excluded—by being aware that their history coincides with that of this God-human who, despite having the dignity of a God, nevertheless cries out like them—recover confidence in themselves. . . . The excluded recognize that they are not alone, that God is with them crying out in unison with them, as God was in the Son. There the power of faith in the one who conquers death on the cross begins to blossom.[9]

Particularly problematic for many is standard atonement doctrine, which asserts that the necessary "at-one-ment" with God (that is, restoring humanity back to the original state of goodness as created in the image of God) required Jesus' bloody sacrifice on the cross. Among those who set forth this key perspective on atonement was the medieval philosopher-theologian Anselm of Canterbury. Pondering why God could not just be merciful and forgive sinners at no cost, Anselm concluded in his famous work *Cur Deus Homo?* ("Why the God-Man?") that it would be "improper" and not in God's nature to do so. God demands obedience, argued Anselm, and disobedience demands punishment or extraordinary sacrifice to satisfy God's law and restore humankind to right relationship with God. Human beings are incapable of suffering adequate punishment or making sufficient sacrifice, reasoned Anselm, concluding, "None but God can make this satisfaction . . . it is necessary for the God-man [Jesus] to make it."[10]

In their extreme, critics of classic orthodox atonement theory ask sharply, "So is your Father-God then a divine child abuser who had to allow or even cause his own Son's brutal ritualistic murder? How could what you call a loving God stand by and do nothing as his beloved Son cried out from the cross in his utter abandonment?" The insightful theologian of the cross Jürgen Moltmann wrote: "That 'God,' the 'supreme being' and the 'supreme good,' should be revealed and present in the abandonment of Jesus by God on the cross, is something that it is difficult to desire. What interest can the religious longing for fellowship with God have in the crucifixion of its God, and his powerlessness and abandonment in absolute death?"[11]

There are no facile answers to these important (and quite reasonable and respectable) questions. To treat these matters adequately, a prolonged discussion beyond the scope of this book needs to ponder God's options in creation, why evil was allowed to enter the good creation, how God's nature requires justice, and what is required for human beings truly to have a large measure of free will and decision-making ability. Even after all those discussions are exhausted, theologians worth their salt will finally conclude, "We do not and cannot know entirely God's ways with the world—especially when it comes to the atonement and the apparent necessity of Jesus' brutal death on the cross—and so they remain a mystery."

What we do claim by faith, received as gift through the power and activity of the Holy Spirit, is that God freely chose to embrace and occupy a one-down position. In Jesus of Nazareth, God became fully human and lived as a common craftsman who at some point in his adult life began to wander around towns and villages as an itinerant teacher and preacher. The common people, in growing numbers, found hope and good news in his teachings. He adopted a servant style of ministry, washing the feet of others, finding ways to provide food and drink to those who had none, bringing a healing touch to those who were suffering. The very notion of a "one-down God" was so offensive to religious leaders and so threatening to civil authorities that he endured a sham trial based on trumped-up false charges. Though convinced of Jesus' innocence, Pontius Pilate lacked the courage to stand up to the masses crying for Jesus' execution, which was a brutal affair carried out to the delight of the bloodthirsty and to the dismay of his followers, most of whom abandoned him in his hour of greatest need.

In the end, however, the Comeback God did not abandon the Beloved Child unto eternal defeat and nonexistence. The same God who anguished but did not intervene amid Good Friday's horrors acted decisively on Easter morning, giving rise to the three-word declaration on which Christianity stands or falls: He is risen!

One-Down with Christ: Clinging to Justification by Grace through Faith

Just as a hospital emergency room may have all the necessary equipment, medicine, and skilled personnel to save my life but is of no avail whatsoever if I cannot walk, stumble, or be carried through its doors, so God's salvation/shalom—achieved through God's self-pouring-out in Jesus' death on the cross—helps not at all if it is not made available to me, to us, to the world, and to the whole creation.

In the most important question ever posed to Jesus, a wealthy young man queried, "What good deed must I do to have eternal life?" (Matt. 19:16-22). This question of *access to salvation*—of how and by whom the door is opened—has been the central issue debated at various points along the way in Christian history and continues to remain at the heart of most great Christological controversies. Jesus' response seemed to imply that some action was required and that salvation could be earned: "Keep the commandments . . . go, sell your possessions, and give the money to the poor." But in his subsequent commentary to the disciples as they wondered, "Then who can be saved?" Jesus clarified that salvation cannot be gained or earned by human action: "For mortals it is impossible, but for God all things are possible" (19:25-26). Paul sought to settle the matter definitively in his great theological declaration regarding justification: "All have sinned and fall short of the glory of God; they are now justified by his grace as a gift, through the redemption that is in Christ Jesus, whom God put forward as a sacrifice of atonement by his blood, effective through faith" (Rom. 3:23-25).

As long as a person grasps for God's favor by means of personal efforts, achievements, or even compassionate self-sacrificial acts of mercy and service to others, she or he will come up short. More than disobedience to God's command in eating the forbidden fruit, Genesis' account of the fall reflects the irresistible human inclination to strive "to be like God." Because of universal human sinfulness, no one can be restored to right relationship with God and others by such striving. And, of course, in the end—when the moment of death finally arrives—we all are incapable of self-conferring the gift of life in the new age with God. So resist it as we may (and we *all* do most of the time!), simple acceptance of the gift of grace is a Christian's and faithful community's most important calling. The great twentieth-century theologian Paul Tillich proclaimed this promise of grace in one of his best-known sermons:

> Grace strikes us when we are in great pain and restlessness. It strikes us when we walk through the dark valley of a meaningless and empty life. . . . It strikes us when, year after year, the longed-for perfection of life does not appear, when the old compulsions reign within us as they have for decades, when despair destroys all joy and courage. Sometimes at that moment a wave of light breaks into our darkness, and it is as though a voice were saying: "You are accepted. *You are accepted*, accepted by that

> which is greater than you, and the name of which you do not know. Do not ask for the name now; perhaps you will find it later. Do not try to do anything now; perhaps later you will do much. Do not seek for anything; do not perform anything; do not intend anything. *Simply accept the fact that you are accepted!*" If that happens to us, we experience grace. After such an experience we may not be better than before, and we may not believe more than before. But everything is transformed. In that moment, grace conquers sin, and reconciliation bridges the gulf of estrangement. And nothing is demanded of this experience, no religious or moral or intellectual presupposition, nothing but *acceptance.*[12]

Long and complicated dogmatic compendia have sought to explicate fully the meaning of this high-sounding doctrine of justification by grace. Two days before his death, in the very last words Martin Luther would write at the end of his prolific literary career, the great reformer prepared to meet God face-to-face: "We are beggars, that is true." Writing of Luther's great insights into this central Christian teaching, Canadian theologian Douglas John Hall warns that especially people of faith may be subject to one-upmanship and have trouble giving themselves over to being rescued in God's holy emergency room of grace:

> To confess "the wisdom of the cross" means, at the most existential level, to know oneself devoid of wisdom. It means being a beggar where understanding is concerned—where life itself is concerned. The gospel of the cross condemns every pretension to possession. It divests man [*sic*] of all he has attempted to use to cover up his essential nakedness. It reduces him to the status of a beggar, robbed, beaten, and naked at the side of the road. Only a beggar can receive the gift of grace. Moreover, he must become a beggar again

and again. His natural tendency is to regard himself as s sufficient, autonomous, master of the situation. Even man of faith—he especially—falls into this habit. He turns faith itself into the stuff that will elevate him above the beggarly condition. He regards himself as growing progressively beyond his beggarly condition. Luther made sanctification and justification almost synonymous, precisely to avoid this implication.[13]

The doctrine of justification is the cornerstone for Christian dogmatic teaching, the balance point on which all theology stands or falls, and the plumb line against which all truth must be measured.[14] This doctrine that for four and one-half centuries appeared to be the chief point of contention and divergence between Roman Catholics and "Protestants" became the rallying place of convergence for a historic Joint Declaration signed in 1999 by high Vatican officials and leaders of the Lutheran World Federation:

> Therefore the doctrine of justification . . . is more than just one part of Christian doctrine. It stands in an essential relation to all truths of faith, which are to be seen as internally related to each other. It is an indispensable criterion which constantly serves to orient all the teaching and practice of our churches to Christ. . . .
>
> We confess together that sinners are justified by faith in the saving action of God in Christ. By the action of the Holy Spirit in baptism, they are granted the gift of salvation, which lays the basis for the whole Christian life. They place their trust in God's gracious promise by justifying faith, which includes hope in God and love for him. Such a faith is active in love, and thus the Christian cannot and should not remain without works. But whatever in the justified precedes or follows the free gift of faith is neither the basis of justification nor merits it.[15]

Where Is Jesus Now? He Has Ascended, Not Abandoned Us!

A predictable question Christians ask is "So where is Jesus now?" The final Christological statement about Jesus in the creeds is that he "ascended into heaven," where the risen Christ "is seated at the right hand of the Father." What exactly might that mean? As in the case of other challenging theological questions we have encountered, the only answer that can be offered is this: It's a mystery shrouded in the veil of eternity that cannot be penetrated by human reason or experience.

Theological reflection on the ascension of Jesus recognizes its inseparability from the resurrection event. The New Testament Gospels do not give uniform witness to a separate postresurrection event that marked the final departure of the risen Christ from earthly apprehension by his followers. Only Luke, with its sequel, Acts, makes unambiguous reference to Jesus' parting or "ascension" (Luke 24:50-52).[16] Both resurrection and ascension are ahistorical—that is, they stand outside history where we can apprehend things that happen in time and can be grasped by human senses.

All we can know with confidence is that the risen Christ—a God-human in continuity with the human-God who was known as Jesus of Nazareth—is alive and ultimately in charge of the universe. While removed from being wholly knowable or fully graspable by our human senses, the Resurrected/Ascended One can be addressed now in prayer and *received* in the high and holy table fellowship of Eucharist or Communion. And in faith we cling to the Comeback One's unambiguous and unwavering promise: "And see, I am sending upon you what my Father promised; so stay here in the city until you have been clothed with power from on high" (Luke 24:49).

In the next chapter, we turn our attention to the nature of this power-clothing third person of the Trinity, the Holy, life-giving Spirit.

For Further Pondering and Probing

1. Many in today's postmodern world argue that archaic terms such as *justification* and *salvation*, seldom if ever used in daily conversation, fail to communicate the gospel. If you agree with Heyward that some "pruning" of doctrine is needed, can you think of more relevant terminology or imagery to convey the good news of God's redeeming actions?
2. One variation of Christology deemed faulty by the broad catholic tradition is called Gnosticism (from Gk. *gnosis*, "knowledge"). This school of thought believes that we are saved through gaining greater and greater knowledge. Gnostic Christology taught that Jesus only appeared to be fully God, because God could never truly inhabit inferior human flesh. Why is it so important that the Nicene Creed declares that Jesus "became truly human"?
3. Just as we have explored the continuing nature of creation, so God's "outpouring" (*kenosis*) did not cease with the incarnation of Jesus. Where in your life, your community, and today's global village do you see signs of God's "pouring it all out" for us?

7

The Spirit's Comeback Community

Pneumatology and Ecclesiology

The church of Christ in every age, beset by change, but Spirit-led,
Must claim and test its heritage and keep on rising from the dead.[1]

THEOLOGIANS LIKE TO INTERSPERSE their lectures and books with what I call "thirty-dollar words." In this chapter I introduce two such theological code words: *pneumatology* (from Gk. *pneuma*, "spirit") and *ecclesiology* (from Gk. *ekklesia*, the "called out"). The first refers to the church's doctrine of the Holy Spirit, and the second to our convictions about the nature of the church.

In both the Apostles' and Nicene Creeds, the third and final articles offer succinct statements about Spirit and church. With regard to the former, the Apostles' Creed states simply that Christians "believe in the Holy Spirit." Nothing more is proffered about the Spirit's nature, powers, or work. The Nicene Creed goes further in asserting that the Holy Spirit is *the Lord* and life-giver; that the Spirit "proceeds from the Father and the Son" and is "worshipped and glorified" (by the faithful) along with the other two persons of the Trinity; and that the Spirit is not new in coming but throughout the ages "has spoken through the Prophets."

Speaking of the church, the Apostles' Creed asserts only that Christians believe in its presence and that it is "catholic," meaning that it is universal, everywhere present where the faithful, the "called out" ones, gather. The shorter creed further declares that the church is "the communion of saints." The Council of Nicea added an additional word with regard to the church, asserting that it is and must be *apostolic*, that is, centered around and in continuity with the true faith passed down through the ages from the hands of the first apostles. This apostolicity must be safeguarded amid ever-present tendencies to water down or go beyond the essentials of the gospel proclamation recorded in Scripture by the gospel and epistle writers.

That these two realities—Spirit and church—are embraced together in both creeds' third paragraphs signals their essential interrelatedness. A Spiritless church would be an empty shell devoid of purpose and power. A churchless Spirit would be inaccessible to us. While indeed the Spirit "blows where [the Spirit] chooses" (John 3:8), and its activities and presence cannot be limited within the bounds of the institutional church, it seems to blow, and tends to hang out most often, in the realm of the church. The one, true, faithful, Spirit-filled church is the most potent force for good ever unleashed in the universe!

The Comeback Spirit: Convincer, Comforter, and Community Organizer

If you want to see church folks become visibly uncomfortable and squirm, invite them into a discussion about the Holy Spirit! For a variety of reasons, the whole area of Spirit-talk or pneumatology engenders more discomfort than most other topics of theology. To be sure, invoking the Holy Spirit can be manipulative or coercive, as when one person in a conflicted conversation declares, "I know I'm right, because the Holy Spirit whispered in my ear last night." Many of us grow uncomfortable when what Paul describes as the "gifts of the Holy Spirit" are mentioned (see 1 Cor. 12–14; Eph. 4–6). The majority of Christians appear not to have been given certain gifts, such as speaking in tongues and the ability to heal or perform miracles. Holy Spirit talk, accordingly, can easily devolve into childish competitive one-upmanship: "I have seven gifts of the Spirit, and you only have three—and even those seem pretty feeble in your case!" Excesses of the so-called "charismatic movement," including this kind of spiritual elitism wherein some Christians seem to wear their spiritual gifts on their sleeves like scout merit badges, have caused conflict and division in some churches.

Our relative comfort or discomfort with Spirit-talk and Spirit-life also appears to depend on cultural dynamics, our "social location," or what psychologists call individual "personality types." Most of us who have grown up in the modern scientific age have worldviews steeped in rationalism. We can explain in cold scientific terms most of what occurs around us. When we switch to talk about a "Holy Spirit" operative in our lives, our faith communities, and the universe at large, we may fear consciously or on a deep unconscious level that we sound like ancients talking about diseases caused by demons rather than germs, or like early astronomers convinced that the earth is fixed at the center of the universe. Perhaps it is time to let the Comeback God bring back a deeper measure of Spirit-presence and move us to greater degrees of comfort with Spirit-talk in our churches.

Returning to our earlier discussion of the Trinity is a good starting point as we seek to develop a richer and more complete pneumatology. As we declare each time we say the Nicene Creed, the Holy

Spirit is nothing more or less than the *Lord* (used most frequently by Christians in describing Jesus, or the "second person of the Trinity") and the *giver of life* (which we probably associate primarily with the Creator, or God in the "first person"). The Spirit is not separate from the other two persons of the Trinity but "proceeds from the Father and the Son"[2] and is inextricably bound up with the other two persons of the Trinity in the ongoing dance of the divine life.

While there are potential pitfalls in utilizing any gender-defined terminology in our God-talk, some persons find it fascinating and helpful to discover that the Hebrew word for "spirit," *ruach*, is a feminine noun. Therefore, it is grammatically appropriate to refer to the Holy Spirit as *she* or as offering *her* gifts to us. One should not make too much of this, however, recognizing that in Greek *pneuma* is a neutral noun and the Latin word *spiritus* is masculine.[3]

Regardless of which particular gifts of the Spirit an individual Christian may possess, the most important gift is bestowed upon us all—belief or faith in the triune God. Christians believe and confess that the Holy Spirit's presence and power are bestowed in the moment of baptism. Following immersion or the pouring of water coupled with the *Trinitarian formula* ("in the name of the Father, Son, and Holy Spirit"), the introduction of the one being baptized into Spirit-life is symbolized both verbally ("You have been sealed by the Holy Spirit") and physically by imposing a cross with blessed oil or *chrism*.

In the great theological treatise that we call the epistle to the Romans, the apostle Paul declares, "When we cry, 'Abba! Father!' it is that very Spirit bearing witness with our spirit that we are children of God" (Rom. 8:15-16). Martin Luther's Small Catechism, accordingly, emphasizes the role of the Holy Spirit as the agent of belief, the one who brings us to conviction and convinces us of the truth of the Christian faith: "I believe that by my own understanding or strength I cannot believe in Jesus Christ my Lord or come to him, but instead the Holy Spirit has called me through the gospel, enlightened me with his gifts, made me holy and kept me in the true faith." Luther went on to underscore the communal nature of faith and the role of the Holy Spirit as a kind of community organizer who brings people of faith together in the one universal body of Christ: "just as he calls, gathers, enlightens, and makes holy the whole Christian church on earth and keeps it with Jesus Christ in the one common, true faith."[4]

Often referred to in the Bible and Christian writings as the Comforter, the Holy Spirit constantly comes back to us in times of trial, offering consolation and courage. When faith is flagging or zeal wanes, the Spirit cajoles us to keep on keeping on. In seasons of sorrow and when a believer begins to feel isolated and alone, the Spirit is a kind of great reminder: "Now remember, my beloved one, you are never alone; not only are we of the Godhead with you, but your sisters and brothers of the human family surround you as well."

The lifelong process of "being made holy" is rendered in the shorthand word *sanctification*. Just as Spirit-talk in general is off-putting for some individuals, so some Christian traditions and contemporary denominations, including those sometimes referred to as "moderate" or "mainline," tend to shy away from the whole concept of sanctification. We who call ourselves Lutherans, for example, are often wary of the topic lest it be misunderstood as just another variation of works-righteousness. Or we suggest that being saved and being Christian are like being pregnant or being married—one either is or isn't—no middle ground and no gradations. Nevertheless, there is a rich tradition of embracing an individual's and a community's growth in grace, godliness, and gratitude. Reflecting a growing embrace of sanctification in recent decades are the increasing numbers of Christian individuals and churches that point to exemplary figures of the past whose lives witnessed to their strong faith commitments. Such revered forebears are often referred to as "the saints."

For those of us who still squirm at the mention of sanctification, or more radically "Christian perfection," as John Wesley and Methodists have labeled it, recognizing its purpose as world-enhancing rather than individual-advancing may be helpful. Ted Peters makes this distinction:

> We do not seek to live lovingly in order to prove ourselves obedient and therefore holy and therefore just and therefore deserving of salvation. In the Reformation tradition we must affirm the sanctifying work of the Holy Spirit, to be sure; but we must affirm with equal vigor that this sanctifying work is aimed at making this a better world and not aimed at achieving the salvation of the believer.[5]

The Church as Believing Body, Mouth House, and Missionary Movement

What constitutes the one true catholic and apostolic church of Jesus Christ? Where does it truly exist? What are its markers? How will we know it when we see it? In pondering matters related to ecclesiology, these are all important questions.

First and foremost, the church is the community of faithful baptized disciples who publicly proclaim (teach) the gospel and thereby call others to be baptized and become disciples. Its constituting mandate was given by our Lord in his final postresurrection instructions to the first apostles, as recorded at the end of Matthew's gospel. Note especially the verbs in the great mission mandate: "*Go* therefore and *make* disciples of all nations, *baptizing* them in the name of the Father and of the Son and of the Holy Spirit, and *teaching* them *to obey* everything that I *have commanded* you" (Matt. 28:19-20).

Among the many New Testament images used to describe the church,[6] perhaps the most compelling and comprehensive is Paul's declaration that the church is the "body of Christ." For Paul the Holy Spirit is the cardiovascular system that enables the body to breathe and live. Yet without physical arms, legs, and other members, a disembodied free-floating Spirit would have no bodily presence in the world. Just as Jesus was the thirty-three-year incarnation of the

Trinity, so the church is the ongoing two-thousand-plus-year incarnation of the Divine One.

Martin Luther had a flair for dramatic description. In one of his cryptic sermonic comments, he zeroed in on one particular part of the body in describing the church as a "mouth house."[7] That is to say that among its many attributes and purposes, the primary mission of the church is to see that the gospel gets spoken in every generation to as many people as possible. The church is to be mouthy in assuring that the Good News ("God raised Jesus from the dead") gets proclaimed. In so doing, the church can trust that, by the ongoing power of the Holy Spirit, this resurrection-proclaiming force is undiminished as time moves along.

Even as it is a mouth house, the one true catholic and apostolic church must also always be a missionary movement. The church does not exist only or even primarily to perpetuate itself as one more institution in society. Rather, the church exists for the sake of the world. It is engaged in God's mission, which, as we have seen, is to heal the wounds wrought throughout history by the forces of evil and restore the whole creation to its original state of true shalom or wholeness.

As Jesus recognized through prayerful dialogue with God the "Abba-Father," in order that the world might believe, the church must be united—that is, it must be *one* (see John 17). This essential oneness of the church has been tested since the very beginning two millennia ago. Early Christian disagreements over who could receive the gospel and what could be required of Gentile believers (see Acts 11–15) foreshadowed later churchly divisions, which led ultimately to the multiple *denominations* we observe throughout the world today. Such fragmentation within the one holy catholic and apostolic church has been ameliorated in some measure by the modern ecumenical movement; yet we have a long way to go in healing the brokenness within the body of Christ. While organizational and structural unity may not be a requisite for true church unity, anything less offers the nonbelieving world a confusing and less-than-convincing witness "that they may all be one" (John 17:21).

God's mission movement, which every community of the faithful is called to join, is holistic and comprehensive. It includes proclamation of the saving Word, worship (adoration and enjoyment of God) that includes the sacraments, service to human need, participation in actions that restore the original goodness of creation, fellowship (celebrating the greatest gift we have—sisters and brothers of the human family who are made in the image of God), and advocacy for and involvement in justice-making. In their great defining document, the Augsburg Confession, the early reformers who came to be called Lutherans summed up these markers whereby one can discern and determine that the true church is present: "It is the assembly of all believers among whom the gospel is purely preached and the holy sacraments are administered according to the gospel."[8] Emphasizing the church's missionary purpose, Anglicans declare in their Catechism, "The Church pursues its mission as it prays and worships, proclaims the gospel, and promotes justice, peace and love."[9]

So often, one or more dimensions of God's holistic saving action are ignored, leading to truncated mission on the part of a community that falls short of its vocational calling. Comfortable middle-class congregations seem particularly susceptible to ignoring altogether or fielding only anemic ministries of service and advocacy for justice. Pietistic and quietist Christians are comfortable with worship, fellowship activities, and a degree of stewardship adequate to keep the wheels of the institutional church turning. It is often among the Christians of the so-called two-thirds world, Latin American and African countries where the vast majority of believers are economically marginalized, that the fullness of mission is exercised in stunning and inspiring ways.

Mission is dynamic, ever-changing, shaped by historical context and social location. A faith community that is attempting to do all things the way they were done decades ago is probably falling short of the mark in fulfilling its mission mandate. Christians who move from one locale to another soon discover that a congregation new to them will feel and act somewhat differently from one to which they previously belonged. Every local manifestation of the wider worldwide body of Christ does well to be in a state of constant prayerful discernment, seeking to read the "signs of the times" in order to discover specific dimensions of mission that need special attention. Such mission-discernment leads to strategic thinking, charting a course and moving along it, all the while attentive to opportunities for spontaneous and unplanned acts of witness and service.

Vocation and Stewardship: Comeback Community Foreshadows the Future

Historically and currently, persons who describe themselves as "having a call" are often presumed to be members of the clergy. Another of Martin Luther's somewhat radical reforming notions was that every baptized Christian has a calling from God. Luther believed further that there is no inherent hierarchy among callings, that to be a farmer or daycare attendant is as important and worthy a calling as to be a priest, pastor, or high church official. In what sounds jarring to many ears today, tainted as we are by the so-called lawyer jokes that run rampant in contemporary society, Luther commented specifically on the Christian vocation of "jurists," noting that their work is to be regarded on an equal footing with that of the clergy:

> Just as a pious theologian and sincere preacher is called, in the realm of Christ, an angel of God, a savior, prophet, priest, servant, and teacher, so a pious jurist and true scholar can be called, in the worldly realm of the emperor, a prophet, priest, angel, and savior. . . . When I speak of the jurists, I do not mean only the Doctors of Laws, but the whole profession, including chancellors, secretaries, judges,

> advocates, notaries, and all who have to do with the legal side of government.[10]

Even as the church universal has a mission—and just as every local expression of the one holy catholic and apostolic church is called to fulfill aspects of that holistic mission—so Luther and others claimed that every Christian is "under call." The Latin word for "calling," *vocare*, is the source of our English word *vocation*. One's vocation, therefore, means far more than occupation or means of earning a living. Indeed, it can be said that Christians have multiple callings or vocations. If married, one is called to the vocation of being a faithful, nurturing, loving husband or wife. If a parent, the vocation of raising children is one of life's highest callings. So, too, is one called to be friend, coworker, and neighbor to many. And yes, one's occupational calling ideally enables the expression of additional dimensions of Christian discipleship.

Another means of viewing Christian vocation is through the lens often called *stewardship*. The biblical understanding of a steward, reflected in several of Jesus' parables as well as in the writings of Paul, is that she or he is one entrusted with the care of property and/or persons who belong to another. A faithful steward-servant is found at all times carrying out the will of the owner-master. According to Jesus, such a good servant will be put in charge of an entire household or estate (Matt. 24:45-51). Likewise, a contemporary steward holds in trust things, relationships, tasks, and responsibilities that are on loan from God for a season. Just as the biblical steward was called to give an account, we must likewise submit a reckoning for how we have fulfilled our stewardship.

As Christian communities "who walk not according to the flesh but according to the Spirit" (Rom. 8:4), congregations and other expressions of the body of Christ are called to order themselves here and now in such a way as to foreshadow the coming reign of God. The writer of 1 Peter pointed to this dimension of a faithful and comprehensive ecclesiology in exhorting early Christians to recognize and act out their existence as "a chosen race, a royal priesthood, a holy nation, God's own people" (1 Peter 2:9). Local Christian communities can offer wonderful laboratories in which to create and conduct experiments in true Spirit-filled life together. In contrast to widespread competitive, oppressive, and adversarial relationships, such faithful communities can strive to embody biblical images such as the lion lying down with the lamb, offering forgiveness seventy times seven, loving and praying for one's enemies, rearranging economic and social life so that the first become last, and stooping to wash one another's feet. In the words of Philip Hefner:

> The idea that the church is transparent to the kingdom of God provides a strong declaration of what the church essentially is, as well as a prescription of what the church must become. . . . Its structures, its message, its liturgy and communal life, and its outreach must always be reformed toward greater conformity with the intentions of God for the world. As the church focuses on these divine intentions and meanings, it renews its ties to the source of its life. The hope of the church points to the day when it will indeed not pass away but will be transfigured in God's own work of consummation.[11]

Of course, both as individuals and as Christian communities, in our vocational callings and steward-service we will always fall short of the fullness God intends and what we ourselves hope to accomplish. It is important for Christian communities to acknowledge humbly that "the church and its distinctive form of life are related to but never identified with the coming reign of God. . . . The triumphalist identification of the church with the reign of God has been the source of much arrogance and destructiveness in church history. The church anticipates and serves the coming reign of God but does not fully realize it."[12] All members of the church "have sinned and fall short of the glory of God" (Rom. 3:23). Accordingly, the church on earth is always a fallen community and will never fulfill completely its vocational calling.

In recognition of the reality that not all who present themselves as faithful Christians are actually committed believers, many theologians have described the church as being a two-faceted community—both *visible and invisible*. The true church—made up of those who have embraced the good news of the gospel and given themselves over to it—is interspersed among a broader visible community that includes individuals who present themselves among the faithful for social respectability or other reasons, but are not truly convicted and committed to the Comeback God's missionary movement.

When faced with the common accusation of being a gathering of hypocrites who fall far short of godliness worthy of true believers, any church does well to respond promptly and unambiguously, "Guilty as charged!" The church awaiting God's final comeback will always be an odd and quirky mixture of saint and sinner, true and make-believe confessors, interspersed visible and invisible realities. We can take heart that for our collective and communal shortcomings there is divine forgiveness. In addition to pardoning others, we can forgive ourselves when we fall short of lofty goals set before us. We can trust that as in a relay race a runner must hand the baton to another, so those who follow after us in the Christian community will take things the next segment of the journey. Among our multiple Christian callings, the stewardship of the Spirit-filled community is paramount. Living gracefully as the communion of saints, "surrounded by a great cloud of witnesses" (Heb. 12:1), we are the *ekklesia*, the "assembly called out" by the eternal life-giving Holy Spirit.

For Further Pondering and Probing

1. The church is often portrayed as a ship, and the main seating area of a worship center is described in nautical

terminology as "the nave." While the image may be useful in conveying the notion of a people in motion toward a destination, a ship is also a self-contained community and not easy to get aboard once launched! What other images of the church do you find helpful?

2. In 1 Corinthians 12:10, Paul notes the importance of "discernment of spirits." Much neglect of duty or outright abuse in the church is perpetrated by those who profess to be "led by the Spirit." Confronted with so many competing "spiritual" claims, how do Christians sort out the wheat from the chaff, the truly spiritual from chicanery?

8

Grace-Filled Continuing Comebacks

Sacraments

You satisfy the hungry heart. . . .
You give yourself to us, O Lord.[1]

GOD HAS GIVEN SOME particularly rich gifts to the comeback community in what are referred to as *sacraments*. The word comes to us from the same Latin origins that give us *sacred*, meaning "holy things." *Sacramentum* literally means "a consecrating," so the sacraments involve common, everyday elements set apart for holy or sacred purposes. The Latin word in turn emanates from the Greek *mysterion*, further deepening the significance of ordinary elements, which, when set apart or consecrated in the community of faith, become holy bearers of divine mysteries and blessings. Our doctrine or theology of the sacraments results in another thirty-dollar word—*sacramentology.*

Within the broad catholic (universal) tradition, there is widespread consensus that the sacraments are "means of grace," channels whereby God's grace is conveyed to human beings through everyday, inexpensive, and widely available physical elements—water, bread, and wine. God has chosen to use these ordinary ingredients to convey deeply spiritual messages and meanings and to effect profound change on the part of those who receive the sacraments. The sacramental elements are physical, tangible, and accessible to human senses—they can be seen, touched, smelled, tasted, and held in one's hand. But while ordinary and highly accessible, they are made bearers of God's spiritual presence.

The sacraments have long been described within Christianity as "outward and visible signs of inward and spiritual grace."[2] A further elaboration is offered by the Lutheran lay theologian Philipp Melanchthon, who defended the Augsburg Confession when he wrote an apology, or defense, for it. The sacraments, he declared, are rites "which have the command of God and to which the promise of grace has been added."[3] Sacramental elements are inseparable from and are *made sacraments* only in combination with the Word of God. Augustine declared, "The word comes to the element and so there is a sacrament, that is, a sort of visible word."[4] In *Visible Words*, Robert Jenson reflects the Augustinian imagery and identifies the nature of the sacramental elements: "God's word is a word with a bath or a meal or a gesture."[5] Beyond being visible, they can be grasped by the other senses as well, as noted by Daniel Migliore in describing them as "palpable enactments of the gospel."[6]

It is when the various Christian communions or "denominations" attempt to go beyond simple definitions that disputes and divisions occur. Some of the historical and contemporary sacramentology disputes center around the *how* questions: How can the risen

Christ who is "in heaven" be truly physically present in the bread and cup of Holy Communion? How can a newborn baby or young child who apparently has little intellectual comprehension receive baptism and its bestowal of membership in a professing community of faith, the church? Other points of doctrinal difference revolve around the *how many* questions: How many "means of grace" did Jesus mandate and promise to infuse with divine sacramental presence? How many times may or should individuals be baptized as they may change from one communion to another? How many times per year or month should Holy Communion be offered and/or received?

Since the author is a confessional Lutheran, what follows will reflect some of the nuances of that tradition within the one holy catholic and apostolic church. While we Lutherans afford sacramental status to only two liturgical actions—baptism and the Lord's Supper or Holy Communion—we honor and consider also as blessings *rites* of the church, that is, other holy activities that other Christians regard as sacraments. We come down to this distinction primarily as a result of the conviction that an essential aspect of a sacrament is its having been mandated by Jesus to be received by all Christians. At his last supper, after taking bread, blessing a cup, and sharing both with his closest followers, Jesus commanded, "Do this." And in his final instructions to the disciples just prior to his ascension, Jesus commanded them to go and make disciples of all nations, *baptizing* them in the name of the triune God (Matt. 28:16-20). Thus, while other parts of the body of Christ regard the rites of marriage, confirmation, ordination or conferring of holy orders, penance (confession of sins), and anointing of the sick (including extreme unction or blessing just prior to death) as having sacramental status, Lutherans and some others do not see these important Christian actions and activities as absolutely essential, required of all Christians, and specifically commanded by our Lord.[7]

Baptism: Born Again of Water, Word, and Spirit

So highly did he regard baptism that Jesus was eager to receive its blessing himself in the Jordan at the hands of John the Baptist (Matt. 3:13-17). In his encounter with the Pharisee Nicodemus by night, Jesus declared, "No one can enter the kingdom of God without being born of water and Spirit. . . . You must be born from above" (John 3:5, 7). For us, baptism in the name of the triune God marks the moment of new birth into life in Christ. Beyond a washing, a cleansing from sin, important as that is, baptism plunges a person into the totality of what may be called the "Christ-event." We are baptized into the death and resurrection of Jesus Christ (Rom. 6). This connection to the events of Good Friday and Easter provides rationale for the historic and current liturgical celebration of baptisms at the Easter vigil, the first annual celebration of the resurrection in many parishes.

Baptism is thus not only being born again in this life, but is birth-unto-eternity. It means being inextricably attached to the Comeback God who has come back from the dead and will one day bring us back into the fullness of life-without-end. In his Small Catechism, Martin Luther asks and answers a central question regarding the sacrament of Christian initiation: "How can water do such great things? Clearly the water does not do it, but the Word of God, which is with and alongside the water, and faith, which trusts this Word of God in the water."[8]

As the church's initiation or entry rite, baptism confers lifelong membership in the body of Christ. Robert Jenson declares, "Whatever the church is or has baptism grants. The repentant can be told: 'You will be saints,' and the baptized told: 'You are saints,' and these sentences are to be taken as *true*."[9] While Christians may continue growing in grace or maturing into what Paul called "the measure of the full stature of Christ" (Eph. 4:13), from the moment of baptism we are full-fledged members of the church. In botanical imagery, therefore, baptism has often been likened to the grafting of a branch rather than the planting of a seed; the former can produce fruit immediately, whereas the latter requires a prolonged period of growth from the point of germination. Theologians Justo Gonzalez and Zaida Maldonado Perez comment on the grafting analogy:

> If baptism is a grafting, it is valid and effective throughout life. When a branch is grafted into the vine—or, in modern medicine, when an organ is grafted into a body—that branch lives out of its constant connection with the vine, of the sap that flows from the roots and which nourishes it. Likewise, if baptism is a grafting into the body of Christ, it is valid whenever, thanks to that graft, the life of Christ flows in us.[10]

While baptism is for life and eternity, and its effects are immediate, full, and complete from the thrice washing with the Word onward, believers have opportunity to daily *live out* and *lean into* our baptism. We are encouraged to remind ourselves frequently of our baptism. Many find helpful such practices as making the sign of the cross, dipping a finger into the baptismal font upon entering a place of worship, or being sprinkled with water in the course of baptismal liturgies. In times when he felt gravely tempted to sin, Martin Luther is reported to have frequently uttered out loud in defiance to the tempter: "But I am baptized!"

A question that continues to elicit differing responses among Christians is "Who then should be baptized?" While all traditions (denominations) seem to concur on its importance, within the larger Christian family, there are two "camps" when it comes to determining the meaning of *faith*, which all deem essential for there to be a true and efficacious baptism. Those broadly termed *baptist* deem it critical that candidates for baptism shall have reached an "age of discretion" at which a considered, thoughtful "yes" can be declared to the questions posed in the baptismal celebration: Do you desire to be baptized? Do you believe in God? and so on. Distinguished from those who follow what is often referred to as "believer's baptism" are the rest of us, Christians who practice "infant baptism" or in other words deem it appropriate to baptize persons of any age regardless of their intellectual or verbal ability to answer for themselves. Fundamental to the distinction is who is deemed to be the primary "actor" in baptism—God or the one being baptized.

Lutherans, Roman Catholics, Episcopalians, Presbyterians, Methodists, and others in the broad liturgical tradition believe that baptizing babies and very small children gives testimony to the radical nature of God's grace, which can be conferred even prior to a person's ability to give verbal assent and offer a personal declaration of faith. At the same time, we do not minimize the importance of receiving and "living out" one's baptismal faith in lifelong fidelity to the triune God. From this perspective, when a person is baptized prior to the age of discretion, the faith community, particularly an infant's parents and baptismal sponsors, makes preliminary profession of faith on behalf of the baptized, which subsequently will be affirmed and ratified in a rite of confirmation or public profession of faith. We deem it pastorally unwise to withhold baptism and its graceful benefits from anyone who is being nurtured within a vibrant Christian community. At the same time, we entrust to God's mercy stillborn babies or anyone who dies prior to Spirit-, Word-, and water-washing, and do not practice baptism of the dead.

We likewise deem it theologically inappropriate to rebaptize anyone already thrice washed or immersed in the triune name of God, as such action would seem to question not so much the faith profession of the baptized as the power of God to adopt and graft into Spirit-life even one incapable of a coherent faith declaration. "God has done it already; don't mess around and try to redo God's work!" is our attitude.

Just as the *who* query regarding baptism is answered differently among Christians, so is the *how*. "Dunkers" and "sprinklers" are names given to the adherents of the two basic methods of baptism. Baptism by full-body immersion appears to have been the practice in Judaism transported into early Christianity. This conclusion is drawn by implication from the site—the river Jordan—where John the Baptist baptized "people from the whole Judean countryside and all the people of Jerusalem" who came to him for baptism, and where Jesus was also baptized. Mark makes it explicit that, following his baptism, Jesus "was coming up out of the water" (Mark 1:5, 10).

At some point in history, Christians began the now-widespread practice of baptizing by pouring a small amount of water over the baptismal candidate's head in a threefold action while invoking Father, Son, and Spirit (the Trinitarian name) as commanded by Jesus. One of the blessings of the so-called liturgical renewal movement of the past several decades has been greater attention to baptismal practice. Liturgical theologian Gordon Lathrop makes a strong case that "the task of the local sacramental assembly is to let the element stand forth in the greatest clarity." Following Martin Luther, Lathrop and many others argue for a return to baptism by immersion "for the sake of the wholeness and integrity of the sign."[11]

Lord's Supper (Holy Communion or Eucharist): A Feast of the Future

As baptism is the church's once-and-for-all rite of initiation, the Lord's Supper or Holy Communion is a continuing celebration and attestation to the reality that God keeps coming back to us and keeps on offering hungry pilgrims spiritual food. Amid the poignancy of what Jesus presumably recognized as his last earthly meal with his beloved disciples, he took bread and broke it, and said, "This is my body, given for you." And then he took a cup of the fruit of the vine and declared, "This cup is the new covenant in my blood, given and shed for you." Urging them to repeat often a similar supper with those same simple elements, he pronounced that each time the faith community reenacted the holy meal, it would be "in remembrance of me" (see 1 Cor. 11:23-25).

The remembering that Jesus offered and mandated was not only of past events. He called upon his disciples (including all of us) to "remember into the future" as well. That is, each time we celebrate the holy supper in Jesus' name and according to his commands and promises, we observe an anticipatory banquet, looking ahead to that future time beyond time when the banquet guest list will be the resurrected ones. Even now, as we reach out empty hands to receive a piece of bread or a communion wafer, and as we grasp a chalice or tiny cup of wine, there are among us the unseen hands of those who have gone on before us into the larger life of God. As we gather to receive our faith food in local believing communities typically called "congregations," so our *communion* extends and embraces the whole church on earth. In the grand feast of the atonement, we are truly made at-one, not only with God, but also with all our spiritual sisters and brothers in every corner of the cosmos.

Throughout the ages, the church has desired to discern and teach its members the benefits bestowed in Holy Communion. The Anglican/Episcopal catechism states succinctly: "The benefits we receive are the forgiveness of sins, the strengthening of our union with Christ and one another, and the foretaste of the heavenly banquet which is our nourishment in eternal life."[12] The Westminster Catechism, a key teaching document for Presbyterians and others, amplifies further the benefits of receiving the Lord's Supper:

> The Lord's Supper is a sacrament of the New Testament, wherein, by giving and receiving bread and wine according to the appointment of Jesus Christ, his death is showed forth; and they that worthily communicate feed upon his body and blood, to their spiritual nourishment and growth in grace; have their union and communion with him confirmed; testify and renew their thankfulness, and engagement to God, and their mutual love and fellowship with each other, as members of the same mystical body.[13]

Martin Luther's Small Catechism declares that in Holy Communion "life and salvation are given to us in the sacrament . . . because where there is forgiveness of sin, there is also life and salvation."[14]

As perhaps in no other area of theology or doctrine, differences and disputes over interpretation of the sacrament of Holy Communion have fostered long-standing feuds and feisty rhetoric. One need only read some of Luther's diatribes against the "papists" or fellow reformers to get a flavor of the neuralgic nature of debates surrounding such matters as "real presence" or whether communicants should receive the sacrament in "both kinds" (bread and wine versus only the former). Much is indeed at stake in how we understand what is going on at the table, who may be called and set apart (ordained) by the church to preside there, and what benefits are bestowed upon us as we receive the sacrament. At the same time as we strive for precision in teaching and interpreting the sacramental experience, however, we also do well to recall its profoundly mysterious aspects, humbly recognizing that none of us can truly grasp its full significance.

A key for many of us contemporary Christians, as it has been all along for large swaths of the Christian family, is the *incarnational* nature of the sacrament of Holy Communion. Just as a few of Jesus' first followers experienced his resurrected presence as they gathered in an upper room (John 20:19ff.) or beside the sea (John 21), so we experience his spiritual and fleshly presence among us as we receive the sacrament of Holy Communion. Luther maintained continuity with the Roman Catholic and Orthodox tradition in insisting on biblical literalism at the point where Jesus declared, "This *is* my body; this *is* my blood." He strenuously opposed those who argued for a mere *spiritual presence* or interpretation that Jesus really meant to say, "This bread and wine represent my body and blood." At the same time, the reformer refused to go too deeply into debates about the physics and chemistry of this *real presence*, not insisting on Roman tradition that asserted actual *transubstantiation* or fundamental change in the elements of bread and wine. For Lutherans, as for others in the Christian family of faith, it is enough to insist that by the power of the Word, Christ's true body and blood are offered in the sacrament, "*under* the bread and wine."[15]

Frequently throughout the course of Christian history, the balance scales that hold in tension Holy Communion as a penitential moment in which the humble sinner is assured of forgiveness over against the sacrament as joyous celebration of thanksgiving (the literal meaning of the Greek *eucharist*) have tipped in the former direction. One observes this in congregations where the time of Holy Communion is marked by hushed silence, long somber faces, and the total absence of any demonstration of happiness, let alone jubilation. Inasmuch as each celebration of the Lord's Supper is indeed a "foretaste of the feast to come," gatherings wherein it is offered should be marked by a spirit of joy and anticipation. Liturgical renewal movements of the past forty years or so have been marked by efforts to liberate the sacrament from a dour piety that enshrouds it in joyless somberness. Afoot in many communions, these renewal movements, which seek to recapture the presumed celebratory nature especially of Jesus' postresurrection gatherings with his disciples, also result in greater frequency of sacramental celebrations. In many congregations today, the prevailing spirit is that espoused years ago by a friend and colleague of mine who declared, "The sacrament is celebrated every time we open the front door of Bethlehem church!"

Coupled with a festive sense of joy and anticipatory excitement in celebrating the sacrament is a profound recognition of its nature as a vector pointing the faithful in the direction of a community marked by peace, justice, equity, and true shalom for all its members. Bradley Hanson insists: "Now we must call attention to the fact that the Lord's Supper is a means of the reign of God. The kingdom or reign of God is a symbol for a situation in which God's rule is no longer opposed but is fulfilled in perfect harmony, peace and justice. . . . This consciousness involves both a recognition of God's judgment upon current injustices and an invitation to strive for a better world and church."[16]

This view of the sacramental meal—as anticipatory communal self-projection into the future shalom-filled reign of God—will suggest to a faith community who ought to be present and even where its feasts may be held. Some of the most powerful witnesses to faith and Christian community today are to be found in unexpected places, as when the meal is celebrated among *campesinos* in remote Latin American villages with children, farm animals, and wild creatures running through the gathered congregation. Or true communion may be observed when the sacrament is offered atop a simple footlocker or jeep's hood by a military chaplain to weary soldiers; or to convicted prisoners who know deep down they are guilty and feel they are unworthy, from the hands of a pastor who is himself an ex-convict. It is particularly as the bread and wine find their way into the hands and mouths and hearts of those who are "the least, the last, and the lost" that true eucharist/thanksgiving occurs and true communion becomes incarnate.

As a concluding note to this chapter on the sacraments, with particular reference once again to the grace-filled continuing comebacks on the part of the God who desires deep and abiding communion with us, a portion of a marvelous global ecumenical document adopted a quarter century ago is proffered:

> As it is entirely the gift of God, the Eucharist brings into the present age a new reality which transforms Christians into the image of Christ and therefore makes them his effective witnesses. The Eucharist is precious food for missionaries, bread and wine for pilgrims on their apostolic journey. The Eucharistic community is nourished and strengthened for confessing by word and action the Lord Jesus Christ who gave his life for the salvation of the world. As it becomes one people, sharing the meal of the one Lord, the Eucharistic assembly must be concerned for gathering also those

who are at present beyond its visible limits, because Christ invited to his feast all for whom he died. Insofar as Christians cannot unite in full fellowship around the same table to eat the same loaf and drink from the same cup, their missionary witness is weakened at both the individual and the corporate levels.[17]

For Further Pondering and Probing

1. Baptism can be described as the "commencement ceremony" in which we are handed diplomas certifying that the curriculum of salvation has been completed. With this diploma in hand, what is the calling of the baptized?
2. For pastoral reasons, some clergy and churches have determined not to require baptism as a prerequisite for receiving Holy Communion. Is such a practice theologically defensible and practically wise?

9

God Comes Back through Us

Ministry

Jesus came and said to them, "All authority in heaven and on earth has been given to me. Go therefore and make disciples of all nations. . . . And remember, I am with you always, to the end of the age.

—MATTHEW 28:18–20

JESUS' PARTING WORDS TO his disciples issued a mission mandate and launched a ministry movement that continues to our own time. As he was leaving his followers (at the ascension), the Resurrected One promised that the Spirit-presence would keep coming back to them. And so it has been for twenty centuries. Each time the church has found itself in danger of perishing—and such times have been legion—the Spirit comes back and raises up courageous women and men who get the gospel spoken, offer leadership to the church, and serve in the public arena as beacons of light pointing to the Light of the world!

We might imagine that God could have chosen to work in other ways to save and redeem, to remind human ones that we are created in God's image and destined for salvation and shalom both in this life and in the larger life of God beyond death. But the creator God, the God of Israel, the God who became fully human in Jesus, determined to work through ordinary people who gather together in the "called-out community," the church.

The mission of the church, as we have seen in chapter 7, is comprehensive and calls upon the community sustained by the Word and the sacraments to be engaged in ever-expanding arenas of outreach, service, and justice-making. Christ's mission was entrusted to *them*—meaning all of them, not just a few select super-disciples. So today the mission of the church belongs to and must be carried out by all of the baptized, not just by a handful of full-time church workers we often call "the clergy." Any theological discussion of ministry, therefore, begins with talk about the ministry of the laity, the *laos tou Theou* or "people of God." While issues surrounding ministry remain controversial and may constitute the greatest hurdles to be overcome as ecumenical unity is pursued, broad consensus among communions was expressed on this matter in the "Lima document" or statement titled *Baptism, Eucharist and Ministry* adopted by the World Council of Churches in 1982:

> The Holy Spirit bestows on the community diverse and complementary gifts. These are for the common good of the whole people and are manifested in acts of service within the community and to the world. They may be gifts of communicating the Gospel in word and deed, gifts of healing, gifts of praying, gifts of teaching and learning, gifts of serving, gifts of guiding and following, gifts of inspiration and

> vision. All members are called to discover, with the help of the community, the gifts they have received and to use them for the building up of the Church and for the service of the world to which the Church is sent.[1]

A person is set apart (consecrated or ordained) for this ministry in the moment of baptism. It was this insight, shocking at the time amid the high clericalism of the late Middles Ages, that led Martin Luther to assert that every Christian is a priest[2]—that is, that there is no hierarchy within which some lord it over others or claim that "my ministry is more important than yours." All are to be involved in proclaiming the gospel, extending the church's ministry into public arenas, and encouraging fellow Christians in their discipleship.

Given the egalitarian nature of ministry that belongs to the whole people of God, there remains nevertheless a unique role for a cadre of Christians who are prepared and called to serve as ordained public ministers. Luther wrestled with this seeming contradiction in his influential treatise *On the Freedom of a Christian*:

> Here you will ask, "If all who are in the Church are priests, by what character are those whom we now call priests to be distinguished from the laity?" I reply, By the use of these words, "priest," "clergy," "spiritual person," "ecclesiastic," an injustice has been done, since they have been transferred from the remaining body of Christians to those few who are now, by a hurtful custom, called ecclesiastics. For Holy Scripture makes no distinction between them, except that those who are now boastfully called popes, bishops, and lords, it calls ministers, servants, and stewards, who are to serve the rest in the ministry of the word, for teaching the faith of Christ and the liberty of believers. For though it is true that we are all equally priests, yet we cannot all, nor if we could ought we, to minister and teach publicly.[3]

Multiple Forms of Ministry Go Back to the Church's Very Beginning

As in all important matters, in determining the nature of the church's public ministry and leadership, Christians seek their guidance first in the Scriptures, particularly the New Testament. Down through the generations of the church, as debates and disputes have arisen over how best to organize for the mission, theologians and other church members have argued their particular points of view on the basis of Scripture. A comprehensive study of New Testament texts that describe leadership in the early church, however, will fail to solve these arguments, for the reality is that a variety of forms of ministry are cited in the book of Acts and epistles of Paul.

After Jesus' ascension, his disciples (who began to call themselves and/or be called by others "apostles"—the "sent ones") returned to Jerusalem, "constantly devoting themselves to prayer, together with certain women, including Mary the mother of Jesus, as well as his brothers" (Acts 1:12-14). It would appear that there was a highly egalitarian communal exercise of mutual ministry. Also indisputable is that women—the first witnesses to the resurrection—were engaged from the get-go! No more need be said in the face of continuing resistance to women's churchly leadership, including ordained leadership, in some communions.

While leadership was shared among the disciples (apostles), the need for coordination by designated "point persons" was apparently recognized. Early in the new community's life, "in those days Peter stood up among the believers" (Acts 1:15). He began to offer guidance, make suggestions, point directions, and identify issues to be resolved, including filling the vacancy among the Twelve left by Judas's defection and suicide. Peter was the chosen or self-appointed preacher on the day of Pentecost (Acts 2:14-40). But Peter was never alone in primacy of leadership; the others "saw the boldness of Peter *and* John" (Acts 4:13). Team ministry was practiced from the outset.

As the fledgling Christian community began to grow, the needs of its members multiplied and could no longer all be met by the original dozen apostles. In order that their ministry would remain centered on missionary proclamation, the Twelve called for an election of the first cadre of deacons, "seven men of good standing, full of the Spirit and of wisdom," who could engage in a primary ministry of service (Acts 6:1-6). In the official commissioning of the initial seven deacons, we find the first reference to a rite of setting apart by the "laying on of hands."

Ministry was getting organized, but not only the apostles or officially set apart servant-deacons were exercising it: "The number of the disciples increased greatly in Jerusalem" (Acts 6:7). Soon, even one who had been the church's chief persecutor—Saul of Tarsus—was overwhelmed by the Spirit. The converted Saul became Paul, a believer and bold missionary committed to extend the gospel outreach "to the ends of the earth," as Jesus had commanded.

Later in the New Testament, 1 Timothy makes reference to bishops and sets forth the qualities the church should expect of those engaged in a ministry of oversight (1 Tim. 3:1-7). 1 Timothy continues with similar expectations of appropriate conduct and comport for those who serve as deacons (3:8-13). These texts are key for those churches that insist on a threefold ordering of the church's ministry, with set-apart cadres of bishops, priests or presbyters, and deacons. Communions that adhere to a "high episcopacy" (from Gk. *episkopos*, rendered as "bishop") deem it essential that the church have bishops in an office of oversight that symbolizes its unity and legitimates or authorizes all others involved in public ministries of Word and Sacrament or diaconal service. Other churches interpret the New Testament scriptures that describe early patterns of church organization or ministry more broadly, seeing a "bishop" as simply the pastor or primary leader of a congregation whose ministry is legitimated by a call from that local community.

We Lutherans, who on this matter might claim for ourselves the middle road or *via media*, regard matters of church organization and ministerial patterns as *adiaphora*, meaning important but non-essential things that can be debated and adapted with flexibility in local contexts. Accordingly, among the current member churches of the Lutheran World Federation, some have bishops ordained in the "historic episcopate," which claims apostolic succession or faithful teaching of the same gospel taught by the first disciples by means of an unbroken chain of the laying on of hands all the way back to that first described in Acts. Those LWF member churches manifest the threefold ordering of ministry, having designated bishops, pastors/presbyters, and deacons. But other member churches have only pastors, some of whom may be elected to serve as presidents or organizational heads of a national church or its subunits.

An Ordained Cadre: The Great Reminders

While many matters of churchly order are *adiaphora* and can be decided so as to best meet the needs of a community at a given time, the vast majority of Christian communions continue in the conviction that a core group of its baptized ministers should be set apart or ordained. Theologian Philip Hefner states the clergy's nature and purpose:

> The *ordained ministry* serves a specific role within this larger ministry, which belongs to God and which forms the substance of the church's ministry. That specific role is to ensure that the church does not forget who it is and what its purpose is. The ordained ministry exists for the purpose of reminding the church in an explicit manner of its nature, goals, and mission. This involves the ordained ministry, first, in teaching, preaching, and presiding over sacramental life; second, in maintenance and governance; and third, in the actual work of caring for people within

> the church (*Seelesorge*) and strengthening them in faith and body so that they can share in the church's ministry. . . . The ordained ministry is monitor, herald, preacher, and proclaimer of the church's identity.[4]

Those of us who are called out and ordained by the church, accordingly, are the "great reminders" in faith communities. We say: "Remember who and whose we are. Remember by whom and why we and the world were created. Remember how we human ones have always fallen short of God's intentions for us, but nevertheless God keeps coming back to rescue and redirect us. Remember that when nothing else would suffice, God poured it all out and gave it all up on the cross. Remember . . . remember . . . remember!"

While all Christians are called into the Word-spreading work of "gossiping the gospel,"[5] the ordained servant cadre bears particular responsibility for careful "text-tending," paying close attention to Scripture and mining from its inexhaustible mother lodes messages and meanings for public proclamation. So central to the work of the ordained is this task of proclaiming Good News that the ordained one frequently is referred to as "the preacher." Through their preaching and teaching, the church's ordained servants equip all the saints for their ministries in daily life. The preachers are the church's practical theologians engaged in the never-ending hermeneutical task (see chapters 3 and 4) of translating the apostolic message into words and images that can be grasped by today's salvation seekers.

The great reminder ministry becomes tangible in sacramental celebrations over which the ordained one (some communions allow lay presidency under extraordinary circumstances) presides. An ordained one normally baptizes, pouring out (or immersing in) water and invoking God's Holy Word to create the bath-unto-eternity. At table fellowship, the ordained one does what Jesus said to do: she or he takes bread, blesses, invokes the Word, and serves the meal in a spirit of gracious hospitality. As Gordon Lathrop sums it up, the church's public ministers are "not ordained . . . to be a caste of Christian princes," but are to "care for the name and the cup of God in the midst of the gathered holy ones."[6]

Holy Order or Functional Servant Cadre?

When people speak or write about ordained ministry, they often describe it in terms of an *office*. Meaning far more than a section of a church building that formerly was commonly referred to as "the pastor's study," this understanding of office connotes a set of responsibilities, duties, and privileges to be carried out in service to and support of the whole church's ministry. In this sense, as an ordained minister I must speak not of "my ministry" as a personal possession or prideful set of accomplishments summarized on a résumé, but as "the ministry entrusted to me by and on behalf of the whole church." This whole-churchly nature of ministry is particularly important to recall in an era of individualism and tribalism. The local tribe (congregation) needs to be reminded continually that it is part of the whole cosmic church catholic, and that therefore its ordained minister(s) does not belong exclusively or even primarily to itself. In this sense, a pastor, priest, or minister will speak of herself or himself as being "a pastor of the Evangelical Lutheran Church in America serving at St. Peter's by the River."

Unlike political or corporate officer posts, the ordained office is not gained by campaign and election or held by self-appointment. One must be *called* to serve in it. The nature of the call is often described as being twofold: internal or spiritual and external or communal (political would be another good word in describing a call that must be issued by the people, or *polis*). One who would serve in ordained ministry surely needs to have some sense or internal feeling of being called by God. But the internal call must be validated by a community (in almost every tradition this extends beyond an individual local congregation to embrace some manifestation of the larger church).

In the author's Lutheran tradition, a "letter of call" (a printed document signed by parish officers and a pastor's bishop) is issued following a congregation's or other calling entity's decision to issue the call. Only upon receipt of the first such official call can a candidate who has completed all educational requirements be ordained. This requirement of an external call's validation of an internal sense of calling safeguards the church against those who may misread God's intentions for their lives or simply be unequipped with a sufficient degree of the many gifts and graces required for effective public ordained ministry.

What are these required gifts and graces? In other words, who may be ordained? A first response is to declare vociferously, "Sinners saved by the grace of God!" The gospel comes to us "in earthen vessels" or "clay jars," and all who are its bearers, including the ordained, remain human beings made of the stuff of the earth. While most Christian traditions hold their clergy to a higher standard than laity (to serve as "models of the godly life"), there must be a realistic recognition that the church routinely and without exception ordains practicing (and hopefully, perennially repentant) sinners. Whatever degree of "Christian perfection" (as John Wesley described the goal of sanctification) may be attained, ordained ministers will remain lifelong imperfect servants.

Just as professions of law, medicine, and other disciplines have their codes of ethics and guidelines for practitioners, so each denomination or church body has its list of standards and desired qualities sought and expected of those who serve as ordained ministers. Common elements include a transparent faith commitment and public profession thereof and the abilities to preach, teach, conduct worship, counsel, and fulfill administrative leadership roles.[7]

In our consideration of sacraments, we noted the age-old disputes over the nature of Jesus' presence in Holy Communion. Does "real presence" mean a change in the substance of bread and wine? Another unsettled debate within the broad church catholic related to ordained ministry holds some similar dimensions in asking whether the one being set apart actually undergoes fundamental change. Those who answer this question in the affirmative may speak of *ontological* alteration, whereby the inner essence of a person is somehow different the moment after ordination than it was the instant before. These more *catholic* (as they are often called) traditions are prone to ordain a person upon completion of seminary or other course of study and prior to actual receipt of a local faith community's call. They view ordination as admitting a priest to lifelong membership in an *order* (akin to being drafted or enlisted in the military) that stands apart from the rank-and-file laity. Traditions with what may be called a "lower clericalism" differ and see the nature of ordained ministry as more *functional.* In this view, one is set apart to carry out specific tasks or functions, but such setting apart does not impose some new altered state of being or induct one into a special priestly order.

As has been claimed in some other areas, here we Lutherans again may come closest to a middle way in our understanding of ordained ministry. With ordination promises not to be taken lightly, one who offers her or his gifts and is recognized by the church's external call receives some unique Spirit-presence in the laying on of hands by veteran ordained ministers, including one who serves as bishop in an office of oversight. Service in the ordained office calls for a high degree of collegiality with peers and shared ministry with and among the calling community—the former collegial body takes on dimensions of an "order" while the latter faith community keeps the ordained firmly planted among the laity.

This doctrine of ministry plays itself out in practical matters related to serving under call. In my denomination, for example, an ordained minister who goes for more than three years without a regular letter of call will typically be removed from the roster of ordained ministers and henceforth is not authorized to exercise the practice of ministry (a *functional* understanding). Yet if that same individual later accepts a call and returns to the practice of ordained ministry, she or he will not be reordained (thus preserving a dimension of honoring an *ordered* concept of ministry). These distinctions get blurred, however, in our denomination's practice of retaining on the active roster retired ministers who may never again step into a pulpit or stand behind an altar. The functional posture that applies to younger "on-leave-from-call" clergy gets set aside in favor of granting honorific continuing clerical status to our retired servants.

A Balanced Ministry: The Church amid Conflict

As we have explored previously, the church as comeback community always lives dialectically, in between conflicting realities: sin and grace, law and gospel, already and not yet. In the words of Jesus in John's gospel, we are in but "do not belong to" the world (John 15:19). As the called-out community, we nevertheless remain embedded in the world amid all the daily turmoil and tensions of life. In such a posture, Christians must be "wise as serpents and innocent as doves" (Matt. 10:16). All who are engaged in the church's ministry, accordingly, must conduct themselves both carefully and courageously, seeking a balanced life that will always be imperfect and unfulfilled in some measure, but that can be satisfying and joyful as well.

One of my seminary teachers, Dr. Eric Gritsch, an immigrant from Nazi Germany who experienced firsthand some of life's atrocities during his youth, wrote of the importance of balancing "servant-hood" and "serpent-hood" while exercising one's ministry:

> The first disciples had to learn what it means to practice both servant- and serpent-hood. . . . Sometimes one must exercise 'tough love,' insisting on what is good for the beloved even when the beloved rejects it. The serpent is the symbol of medicine; surgery is the exercising of tough love on the physical body. . . . The serpent-hood of the saints is very often rational cold-bloodedness for the sake of caring for the neighbor.[8]

The church—as both congregation and inclusive communion—often suffers deeply and unnecessarily because its ministers, both lay and clergy, are unable or unwilling to break out of a posture of "terminal niceness." All manner of mischief is sometimes tolerated, because to confront and hold persons accountable for their destructive and community-damaging behavior would not be nice or might even appear unforgiving and unchristian.

Those called to leadership in the church are called to reflect deeply and theologically about their callings, which often include boundary-setting disciplinary measures with destructive-prone individuals for the sake of the well-being of the entire community. Such theological reflection ponders the lifestyle of Jesus, wherein our Lord seemed to be frequently in conflict with persons and principalities bent on dominating and one-upping others. As he held in check the destructive behaviors of those seeking to be one-up, he simultaneously beckoned the one-downers of his time, "Come on back now. Remember, we—all of you and I—constitute the comeback community!"

The words of Paul suffice to summarize the purpose and nature of this chapter on the doctrine of ministry: "To know nothing among you except Jesus Christ, and him crucified" (1 Cor. 2:2)!

For Further Pondering and Probing

1. The Roman Catholic Church has a very "high" doctrine of ordained ministry, which includes the claim of "infallibility" when the pope makes certain declarations. By contrast, some Christian communities are entirely egalitarian and have no designated set-apart leaders or clergy. What are the theological foundations for and practical implications of such widely diverse understandings of "ministry"?
2. In what is referred to as the "power of the keys," a pastor declares forgiveness of sins "as a called and ordained

minister of the church of Christ, and by his authority."[9] What are the pastoral implications of the "power differential" established by such authority? Theologically, does God truly push the "delete" key and erase all divine memory of individual sins? How can this be reconciled with God's demand for justice and restitution when others have been harmed by a sinful action?

10

Awaiting God's Final Comeback

Theological Ethics

Every call of Christ leads us into death!

—Dietrich Bonhoeffer

IN THIS BRIEF BOOK'S final chapter, we come full circle, looping back to the beginning where we started at the end. Writing this final chapter in the season of Advent, I am drawn to an image by Letty Russell, whose own advent into the larger life of God occurred just months ago. In *The Future of Partnership*, the late pioneering feminist theologian wrote of the "advent shock" experienced when one recognizes that the way things are is not the way they should be: "Because of advent shock we seek to anticipate the future in what we do, opening ourselves to the working of God's Spirit and expecting the impossible."[1]

Expecting the impossible is an act of praise. When we worship, we say and sing radical and seemingly ridiculous things like the following:

This is the feast of victory for our God,
For the Lamb who was slain has begun his reign.
Gather the hopes and dreams of all;
Unite them with the prayers we offer.
Grace our table with your presence,
And give us a foretaste of the feast to come.

Lord, now you let your servant go in peace;
Your word has been fulfilled.
My own eyes have seen the salvation
Which you have prepared in the sight of every people.[2]

Theological Ethics as Praise, Prayer, Politics, and Praxis

If we really believe it when we make such outlandish claims, if we truly understand our worship as a feast of victory—a foretaste of an even greater feast to come—and actually know that our eyes already have seen salvation/shalom (even as we simultaneously comprehend deep in our bones that it has not yet come in all its fullness), then our praise is inseparable from our politics. That word comes, as we saw previously, from *polis*, the Greek word for "people." Because we believe that God who created *all* people loves and cares for us all, we cannot help but be drawn into political (that is, people-oriented) action. The attempt to ensure that such action be right action—that it do more good than harm and that it be in accord with God's plans and purposes—draws us into the arena of *theological ethics*. Ethical reflection begins "by asking what our lives are for. . . . Why have we been created? For what purpose? What ends are we to serve?"[3]

The word *ethics* comes from the Greek word *ethos*, meaning character or custom. So *ethics* means the whole collection of customs (actions and their underlying guiding beliefs and driving forces) that marks a person or community. According to common dictionary definitions, it refers to a set of principles of right conduct and/or a theory or a system of moral values. For Christian theologians, it is appropriate to speak of theological ethics to distinguish this field of reflection from philosophical or purely humanistic ethical deliberation. Theological ethics is God-centered. We approach questions of right conduct not simply by asking what is congruent with our personal and communal values, but with the serious quest to determine "What does God desire?" Those of us who seek to conduct our politics in congruence with our praise are in search of ethical perspectives and conduct that reflect the Comeback God's compassion and Christlike service and advocacy for justice.

Theological reflection about an appropriate Christian *ethos*, to be embodied in personal actions, decisions, and lifestyle, as well as in our communal life together, can begin at any number of starting points. The theology of creation (see chapter 2) reminds us that our actions can be in response to God's generosity, marked by grateful stewardship in caring for the whole creation, and especially for our sisters and brothers in the human family.[4]

Pneumatological perspectives (see chapter 7) call us into discernment of the Spirit's leading and the quest for how our words and deeds might be life-giving rather than death-dealing. The fullest Christian ethical reflection is generated at the Christological center. Accordingly, let us root the remainder of this discussion in the theology of the cross and consider the nature of *cruciform* Christian ethics. Just as the dying heart of Jesus was at the intersection of two crossbeams—one horizontal, pointing outward at the whole creation, the other vertical and locating the crucified Jesus literally between heaven and earth—so at the heart of Christian ethics are several twofold intersecting dialectics: creation and redemption, saint and sinner, law and gospel, already and not yet, realm of the new age and realm of this world.

As Martin Luther's history-changing Ninety-five Theses crescendo to their finale, the great reformer establishes himself as a thoroughgoing theologian of the cross: "Blessed are those prophets who preach to God's people, 'the cross, the cross,' where there is no cross!" Luther contrasts a theologian of the cross with the theologian of glory. The theologian of the cross speaks the truth in love, names evil, and points toward forgiveness and newness of life in the crucified Christ: "Thus, it is only in Christ crucified where we find the true theology and true knowledge of God, as is set forth in John 10: 'No one comes to the Father but by me'; 'I am the door/way' etcetera."[5]

The cross that took the life of Jesus of Nazareth was planted with a universe-shattering thud in the earth on a hillside outside Jerusalem in a place called Golgotha. The earth itself—our life-giving home and habitat—was used by the forces of evil as an execution theater. As Paul wrote so eloquently, "The creation was subjected to futility" and "has been groaning in labor pains," waiting eagerly to "be set free from its bondage to decay" (Rom. 8:18-23). Cross-centered ethics, therefore, is redemption-yearning. Reflecting the grand tradition lifted up over and over again in the Hebrew Bible, it is also justice-seeking: "And what does the LORD require of you but to do justice, and to love kindness, and to walk humbly with your God?" (Micah 6:8).

Try as we might to be obedient, however, we inevitably fall short in our efforts to live faithfully. Martin Luther, in his theological anthropology or doctrine of humanity, said that Christians are always *simul justus et peccator*—justified, redeemed, and sanctified saints, and power-grabbing, selfish, destructive sinners at the same time. Given our inevitable sinful shortcomings, accordingly, our approach to ethics should always be marked with a degree of humility and some tentativeness. We should begin many of our assertions by saying, "I could be wrong, but this is how I see it."[6]

In recognition of our own individual limitations and tendencies to be *incurvatus in se* (turned in upon ourselves), a cruciform ethic is of necessity communal in nature. That is, while recognizing and supporting the freedom of individual conscience (remember Luther's bold declaration, "Here *I* stand!"), we do well to balance personal ethical actions by constantly testing our beliefs and conclusions with those of others. "Here is how I see things and what I believe must be done; now what am I missing or where might I be wrong?" is a good two-pronged question to pose in communal dialogue. Faith communities—congregations, larger denominational and ecumenical gatherings, and even interfaith dialogues—can and must become increasingly what my denomination has described as "communities of moral deliberation."[7]

Cruciform Ethics: Life in Two Realms

Beginning with Augustine, who wrote of the "Two Cities" of God, there is a long theological tradition of considering ethical matters within a framework frequently referred to as the two kingdoms (also, realms or ages) theory. Recognizing that we live in the realms of both law and gospel, in our still-sinful shortcomings and as already-redeemed saints, God has found it fit to deal with us in these "in-between times" via a twofold response. In the eschatologically determined realm (the new age), God responds with the gospel; in the still sin-bound realm (this age), God orders things by means of law. The church as community in both ages lives in this tension. We offer God's forgiveness, and we hold persons accountable for their actions and exert discipline when necessary.

A contemporary example of a church living in both realms can be found amid the tragic circumstances that have come to light in the past two decades as story after story emerges of children and adults (the majority women) sexually abused by a minister or priest. Frequently, in the past when such revelations of abuse were presented, ecclesiastical authorities rushed to forgiveness out of the conviction that only gospel-realm responses were appropriate. In more recent times, as a result of courageous work primarily by pioneering women leaders, the response has come to include holding perpetrators accountable for the damage they have done. A church that is holding *both* God's hands of law and gospel says to its perpetrators of abuse: "While we can and must offer God's forgiveness and promise of eternal salvation, at the same time we must withdraw God's and the church's sanction of your ministerial privileges and remove you from the office of public ministry." Similarly, a church true to its two-realm ethical convictions may extend God's forgiveness to convicted criminals while simultaneously standing with the state in upholding fair sentencing and appropriate punishment imposed by courts acting justly.

Much confusion surrounds two-realm ethical principles when it comes to the appropriate role for Christians as citizens in the civil order. Many distort the theory and claim an absolute "separation of church and state" to the point of isolationism and withdrawal. Such Christians believe that the faithful cannot allow their hands (and souls) to be tainted by civic and political involvement. At the other extreme are theocrats who would dissolve the two-realm tension entirely, convinced that the call of God is to "take over" the civil realm and impose Christian values and their personal Christian convictions on the entire society. An appropriate two-realm ethic again positions us right in the middle where we seek to live out our faith-centered values and convictions in the civil realm, debating, voting, even running for and serving in public office, but always with the recognition that others of other faiths (or no faith) have equal rights to exert their influence.

The status of church-state relations carved out in the United States by this republic's founders is accurately described as one of "institutional separation and functional interaction." That "Congress shall make no law respecting the establishment of religion, or the free exercise thereof" (U.S. Constitution, First Amendment) ensures the former; that all citizens are imbued with "inalienable rights" (Declaration of Independence), which include the right of civic involvement and the benefits of civil services, guarantees the latter.[8]

Commenting on the nature of moral deliberation and churchly decision making when it comes to the challenging and complex issues we face at any moment while living in two realms, Gerhard Forde writes:

> How does the church which has heard [the gospel] decide what to do? It uses its head and its heart in the concrete situation, to attempt to incarnate the commandment of God. In this task the church can and must utilize all the wisdom of its own tradition and experience as well as the wisdom of the world. In seeking answers in concrete situations to the question "What should we do?" the church can draw on the work of the wise of all ages, the specialists who can help in seeking to apply the commandment of God to take care of the earth and the neighbor in complex and changing situations.[9]

Law under Gospel: Christian and Churchly Civil Disobedience

Paul taught his fellow early Christians to respect and obey the civil authorities, as well as the laws of nature (Rom. 13:1-7). Later Christian teachers and preachers followed suit in the recognition that in the realm of this age, God uses natural and civil law to order society and inhibit living beings from destroying each other in a random, chaotic cosmos.[10] Throughout the centuries, most Christians have found it possible to live most of the time within the bounds of laws enacted and enforced by their governments. Some have chosen to set themselves apart in close-knit communities (ascetic groups in early Christianity, monks in the many monasteries that sprung up during the Middle Ages and still exist in smaller numbers, and contemporary groups like the Amish and Mennonites). But even these who self-select or are born into such cloistered communities must interact with the larger outside world from time to time, and they generally do so in ways that respect and are in conformity with civil laws.

From time to time, however, faithful Christians come to the conviction that to be true to the gospel they must disobey unjust law and challenge or even seek to overthrow demonic civil governors. As was noted in the chapter on Scripture, the book of Revelation is "written in code," and many references to the various beasts can be understood as pointing toward an oppressive Roman regime that increasingly was persecuting Christians. It has been suggested that, in response to rigid legalists who insist on the basis of Romans 13 that Christians may never challenge duly elected civil authorities, that passage must be held in dialectic tension with Revelation 13, a thinly veiled encouragement to question and perhaps even disobey unjust Roman rulers.[11]

Numerous examples can be cited of heroic Christians who came to the conclusion that faithfulness to the gospel required civil disobedience. Many of the early Christian martyrs (the word itself means "witness" and the martyrs' witness extended all the way to offering their very lives in order to remain faithful) were killed because of perceived or real acts and attitudes of disobeying laws and civil authorities. If complying with a law or mandate meant denying the faith (*apostasy*), those courageous Christians said a bold and firm "no," prepared to pay the ultimate consequence. More contemporary examples also provide compelling stories of faithful disciples who challenged governing authorities to the extent that they were executed. German Lutheran pastor Dietrich Bonhoeffer, whose ethical reflection caused him to join in a plot to assassinate Adolf Hitler, was arrested, imprisoned, and hanged to death shortly before the end of World War II.[12] Similarly, the courageous action of

Archbishop Oscar Romero in standing up to a brutal government in El Salvador during the 1970s resulted in his assassination while celebrating Holy Communion in the chapel of a home for the elderly where he had taken up residence.[13]

A current ethical issue with which many nations are struggling, and about which Christian congregations and communions are in hot debate, is that of appropriate responses to burgeoning numbers of migrant peoples, many of whom are undocumented, having crossed national borders without proper immigration papers. Euphemistically they are often called "illegal aliens," even though they have not been convicted and according to American principles of justice, one is innocent until proven guilty. Many of us join Holocaust survivor Elie Wiesel in refusing to use this terminology and asserting that "there are no illegal human beings."

How shall we respond—as individuals and congregations and as a nation—in the face of this "sea of humanity" that is among us, in many cases unprotected by laws and not afforded benefits available only to citizens and other legal residents? The author faced this question directly during the years I served as pastor of a bilingual congregation in California. I readily determined it was not my role to ask for "green cards" at the altar of Holy Communion! The congregation caught its own vision of being a place of "sanctuary" and on numerous occasions has said a polite but firm "No, you may not enter" when immigration authorities have been in pursuit of individuals who sought refuge on church property.

Another perennial ethical issue for Christians involves the use of violence, generally expected as a measure of last resort on the part of those who serve in military forces. Some Christian traditions (often called "peace churches") have carved out an unambiguous antiwar stance and expect their adherents to be "conscientious objectors" when it comes to military service. Other communions leave such decisions to individuals and will offer support both to conscientious objectors and to those who determine their Christian calling (vocation) is to serve in the armed forces. Still other churches seem to have adopted a form of "civil religion" that makes no distinction between the reign of God and their particular nation or country. "Do whatever is necessary to protect and defend our country" would be the attitude of adherents of this extreme nationalistic stance.

Ethical Decision Making: A Communal Prayerful Praxis

While many theological issues have proven conflictive and even church-dividing, it may be the case that our greatest fights within the one holy catholic and apostolic church center around ethical issues and moral stances. In the current era of global Christianity, newspaper headlines feature church fights over homosexuality, immigration-related issues, and other ethical questions far more than about respective doctrines of the Eucharist or varying Christologies. Ethical matters, it would seem for many, "where the rubber hits the road" in determining whether an individual, congregation, or church is *really Christian*. Because so much is at stake, in terms of a particular ethical issue itself, as well as the unity of the church and our public witness, the way in which ethical decisions are made by an individual or Christian community is crucial.

As in all theological reflection, considering how our Lord made decisions is a good place to start. A first marker of Jesus' decision making was his *prayerfulness*. Time and again, Jesus went off alone or in the company of his small band of disciples to pray. Multiple passages in the New Testament describe him as being in prayer "all the night long" or for extended periods. Even as he frequently went apart on his own to wrestle with his conscience and beseech his Abba Father, Jesus was also in constant *communal* dialogue with his closest followers and with a broad general public, including groups and individuals who opposed him—especially the Pharisees and other religiously fervent folk of his day. This mode of communal decision making was embraced by the early church as it quickly adopted a *conciliar* style of gathering representatives from emerging Christian communities for prolonged, prayerful discussions of important vexing issues.

Finally, our Lord's decision making seemed to strike a *balance* between maintaining good order in the public arena (Jesus was by no means an antinomian who flaunted the civil law) and addressing the needs, hurts, and struggles of individuals who placed themselves in his pathway. In this regard, Jesus recognized the *relativity* of laws and cultic regulations. He concluded that laws prohibiting healing or responding to someone's grave need on the Sabbath are not absolutely binding, whereas obedience to the second greatest commandment ("Love your neighbor as yourself") is not optional.

Reflection on Jesus' lifestyle and ethical decision making, as well as consideration of how the early church approached challenging issues, would suggest that the paradigm of congregations and other church gatherings functioning as prayerful communities of moral deliberation is a good one. How such communities carry out their deliberation also becomes very important. As churches of the twenty-first century are "living into" moral deliberation and ethical decision making amid ever-growing complexities and ambiguities, new ecclesial lifestyles seem to be emerging in some quarters. Many deliberative bodies (synods, presbyteries, sessions, or whatever such local and wider groups call themselves) are recognizing the limitations of yes/no, up/down votes where deeply complex and multifaceted issues get resolved by narrow votes, dividing a community into winners and losers. While deliberation and decision making by means of parliamentary procedure may be required in large gatherings of thousands, many smaller communities are in search of alternative methods that involve processes more conducive to *discernment* rather than crisp and efficient decision (the latter word means "to cut," and decision making often unnecessarily severs "losers" from their beloved communities).[14]

Latin American and other "theologians of liberation" have employed a term rich in complexity—*praxis*—to summarize communal ethical reflection, decision making, and action. To describe praxis as *theological reflection upon the actions of individuals and communities engaged in a liberative lifestyle* only begins to unveil the multifaceted richness of this word. "Praxis-based theology is characterized by an ongoing, dynamic, and complex relationship between the concrete social context and theological reflection," conclude Susan Thistlethwaite and Mary Potter Engel.[15] Cruciform theological ethics calls us to ally ourselves with forces of healing and justice making, to act and reflect, then act once again.

Prayerful praxis at the intersection of praise and politics moves the Christian community forward in history, giving special attention to those on the margins, as we *live theology* from the underside. As we march onward, we can be confident that the Comeback God simultaneously moves toward us from out of the future, promising, "And remember, I am with you always, to the end of the age" (Matt. 28:20).

For Further Pondering and Probing

1. As noted in the chapter, there is a distinction between core theological or doctrinal teachings and ethical positions and actions. Significant deviation from core tenets of the gospel may be church-dividing, whereas coming to different conclusions about "right doing" as Christians need not cause such division. How does one distinguish a "core belief" from a matter of ethics? (Some exploration of the concept of *status confessionis* will be helpful in this further probing.)

2. As witnessed in corporate scandals, politicians' illegal activities, and clerical misconduct of recent years, self-delusion is often at the heart of ethical misbehavior ("Yes, I understand the rule/law, but I'm special and 'above the law' that must be obeyed by everyone else.) What theological-anthropological (doctrine of humankind) convictions can help Christians avoid going astray? What are some practical ways in which the "communal prayerful praxis" described at the end of this chapter can take place?

A Concluding Personal Postscript
Grave-Merry Life in the Meantime[1]

AS I COMPLETE THIS short Christian theology primer, the days of Christmas are upon us. In these final days of the Advent season, sounding all around at worship and even in some secular settings are hymns and carols that promise "Emmanuel—God with us." Arriving daily through the front door mail slot are Christmas cards reassuring us that Christ comes again this season, as he came lowly and in a manger two thousand years ago. A few of the holiday greeting cards even bear bold eschatological predictions pointing toward the future great comeback scenario when the resurrected crucified God will say one more time, "All is finished." Sunday worship readings underscore these Advent promises that "God has something up God's sleeve that we ain't seen the likes of yet"![2]

Amid the holiday season hustle and bustle, I am reminded of an earlier Advent in my childhood when I experienced a shocking and delightful recognition that "there's more out there than I ever realized." Because my parents stewarded a herd of dairy cows, whose twice-daily swelling udders had no interest in the notion of vacation or days off, we rarely took any family trips beyond an hour's drive from our little farm in western Minnesota. It was almost impossible for my father to get away from his unrelenting chores for more than a few hours. But I do have vivid memories of one November when my brother was left in charge at home and my parents and I made the big trek to "the cities" (Minneapolis–St. Paul) for Thanksgiving with my godparents. Back in those days, the big downtown Minneapolis department stores like Dayton's debuted their supersized Christmas window displays on Thanksgiving night, and we joined thousands of others downtown ("in the loop") that year for the extravaganza. I was simply dazzled to behold both miniature and life-sized portrayals of all manner of Christmas scenes, made possible with big-city resources that far out-scaled the decorations in our small rural communities.

The gospel, the Good News, the story of the Comeback God and that God's interactions with the cosmos, is what Christian theologians attempt to convey through the windows that we create with words. We hope that on occasion our word pictures of complex concepts elicit a response similar to mine some five decades ago: "Wow! I had no idea such wonder and beauty are out there in the larger world!" It is my hope that the ten chapters in this book not only have offered information, but on occasion may have conveyed a sense of awe, created excitement, and fostered eagerness to imagine just what might be up God's sleeve in the days, years, and eons to come.

We who have hitched our wagons to the star that led earlier salvation-seekers to a manger, and who have staked our futures on the claims and promises coming to us from the God who promises ever and always to keep on coming back among us, continue to live on in these in-between times. In between creation and culmination, in between good and evil—both manifest in full measure all around us—in between God and the teeming masses who most of the time seem to live a-theologically (neither atheists nor agnostics, so many simply seldom give much thought to divine matters), we live out our callings.

"How should we then live?" asked the evangelical scholar Francis E. Schaeffer three decades ago in a widely disseminated book and video series bearing that title. That question always arises sooner or later in theological conversations. For a life of faith is not just a matter of belief, but of attitude and action.

A study of the history of religions, and even of Christianity, reveals that for so many adherents to a particular faith, that spiritual way is perceived as guaranteeing an escape from this world filled with so many struggles and so much suffering. But the God who became incarnate in Jesus embraced and "took on" the world with all its joys and pains, wounds and wonder. And this Comeback God promises to keep on coming at, for, and into the world, day after day after day. "The true God," says Robert Jenson, "is the one coming as the future rushes upon us." This Comeback God, in whom we believe, "is life rather than release from life."[3]

As we—you the reader and I the author—have explored together many of the key themes and theologies that contribute to the current comprehensive global Christian and human conversation, time and again the importance of examining or exegeting one's *context* has been lifted up. To be Good News in a given time and place, any God-word or theological statement must be addressed to people in their context. Our current situation may be summed up in many ways, but a few common themes keep recurring. We are increasingly a global village interlinked by rapid transit and wondrous instantaneous communications technology. Despite the possibility of knowing each other more readily and deeply, however, estrangement, fragmentation, and fear of those who are different seem to be on the rise. Rather than diminishing, the disparity between rich and poor is ever on the rise. While there has been some significant expansion of opportunities available to women and people of color, misogyny and racism flourish in many places. Although the threat of global holocaust by nuclear weapons may have subsided a bit with the ending of the so-called cold war, global warming increasingly threatens the very inhabitability of our earthly home. In short, the times remain turbulent. Anxiety and fear build daily. But for Christians, our time, like every time, is above and beyond all else God's time! The Christian's calling in these turbulent times is for courage, not comfort, for conviction, not complacency.

Describing Pope John XXIII, German Jesuit theologian Hugo Rahner characterized the winsome, popular pontiff as being "God's grave and merry person." As theologians of the cross who, in Luther's words, "call a thing what it really is"; as persons of courageous faith who look deeply into the wounds of the world, we are certainly possessed of a sense of gravity. But balancing this gravitas is a lighthearted merriness flowing from the recognition that the Comeback God always walks beside us and, at the same time, awaits us just up ahead on the journey.

Addendum
How Theologians Work

Method

ONE OF MY COLLEAGUES, who is acknowledged in the preface as a reader of this book in draft manuscript, wisely advised against including this final segment in the body of the text. He counseled that many newcomers to theology would slam the book shut and never reopen it if this section was included! Given my colleague's good advice, I removed this section from the chapters. Nevertheless, I am convinced that even a foundational theological primer should include a brief description on how theologians go about their work. Those who have read the book to its conclusion and who now delve into this final addendum, or "added word," might consider themselves granted a measure of extra credit.

In "doing theology" ourselves, we need to be self-aware of how we approach the task and how our approach will to some degree influence or even predetermine the outcome of our investigations. In this addendum, accordingly, we turn our attention to what is often referred to by theologians simply as *method*. Seeking to define and describe it, theologian Daniel L. Migliore writes:

> Theology not only asks questions but must be self-conscious about the way it does so. This is, in brief, the problem of theological method. While much has been written about theological method in recent years, we are far from any clear consensus. No doubt differences in theological method reflect fundamental differences in understandings of revelation and the mode of God's presence in the world. They also show the limitations of any single method to do all the tasks of theology.[1]

Just as no two surgeons perform an operation in exactly the same way, or no two pilots fly an aircraft from departure to destination in precisely the same manner, so it could be concluded that there are as many theological methods as there are theologians. Nevertheless, as in most matters, it is possible to distill from the infinite number of approaches to God-talk some overarching patterns and broad generalizations. In this description of methods, a baker's dozen will be described.

The great Swiss theologian Karl Barth's name is perhaps the most frequently associated with what is often referred to as the *Christocentric* method, also called the *theology of the Word of God*. The Barthian approach to theology begins from a fundamental conviction that God can be known only as God self-reveals through the divine Word, which is seen most clearly in Holy Scripture or the Bible. That Word is Jesus Christ, so all theology is grounded in and founded upon the apostolic witnesses to the significance of Jesus' life, teachings, death, and resurrection. Summarizing the Barthian method, Migliore writes, "Theology for Barth is the process of subjecting the church and its proclamation to questioning and testing by reference to the living Word of God in Jesus Christ."[2]

Closely related to the Word-centered method is what might be called an *exegetical-homiletical* approach. This is the preacher's method of embracing a portion of Scripture (often described by the Greek word *pericope*, meaning "a cutting" or excerpt) and drawing from it theological meanings to be presented in a sermon, lecture, or Bible study. A proclaimer of God's Word assumes an awesome task whereby she or he seeks to re-present the authentic gospel first spoken by Jesus' apostles in such a way as to be understood by her or his listeners. In other words, the practicing theologian seeks to be "both reverent and relevant."[3]

Those who organize key theological themes and principles for presentation to new converts or persons growing in the faith are utilizing what might be called a *catechetical* or *pedagogical* method. Martin Luther's small and large catechisms and the Westminster Catechism are examples of this approach to God-talk. They set forth primary teachings on topics such as the creeds, sacraments, meaning of the Ten Commandments, and Lord's Prayer.

An expanded and more extensive version of the catechetical approach results in what is sometimes referred to as the *confessional* method. The so-called Lutheran Confessions contained in a comprehensive volume entitled *The Book of Concord* are an enduring exposition of Christianity as understood by sixteenth-century reformers who came to be known as Lutherans.[4] Confessional theologians think, teach, and write out of a particular tradition (or denomination) and seek to set forth its tenets. While there may be many factors that define a Christian as Lutheran, the key to such self-identity is that one sees himself or herself as being in assent with at least the broad overarching interpretations set forth in the Lutheran confessional documents.

Down through the centuries, some of the greatest theologians have not been regarded as such by themselves or others. The church's hymn writers, through what might be termed the *doxological* method, have shaped faith development more broadly than perhaps any other group of theologians. The psalmists who wrote the grand songs recorded in the Old Testament were doxological theologians attempting to set forth God's will and ways with the universe in their exquisite verses that were set to song. Contemporary songwriters continue adding to the rich theological corpus of the church's theology in music.

A variation of doxological method is that which might be entitled *devotional* or *meditative*. The worldwide publication of thousands of resources and aids for personal and communal devotional activity—in books and pamphlets and increasingly through electronic means of delivery—constitutes another rich theological corpus of material developed by both "professionals" (clergy and professors) and "amateurs" (that is, people who do not make their living as theologians).

A theological method described as *correlation* is associated most often with the great twentieth-century German-born theologian Paul Tillich. In the first volume of his *Systematic Theology*, Tillich described his method, which he also calls "answering theology":

> The method of correlation explains the contents of the Christian faith through existential questions and theological answers in mutual interdependence. . . . In using the method of correlation, systematic theology proceeds in the following way: it makes an analysis of the human situation out of which the existential questions arise, and it demonstrates that the symbols used in the Christian message are the answers to these questions. . . . The Christian message provides the answers to the questions implied in human existence.[5]

Upon the broad scaffold of correlational theology, a variety of subcategories can be found, depending in great measure upon the analytical tools employed in asking questions. A *philosophical* method frames the existential questions primarily using the language of philosophy. Tillich proceeds along the philosophical pathway when he uses metaphors such as "ultimate concern" or the "ground of being" in his *Systematic Theology*.

Scientific approaches to the theological enterprise have been launched in recent years; these methods turn to scientists, particularly astronomers and cosmologists, for example, in raising fundamental questions about creation. Still further subsets of scientific method can be delineated; for example, a *psychological* or *psycho-social* approach would frame profound theological questions utilizing categories of human development and small group dynamics.[6]

As we explored in chapter 3, any theological work occurs within and is shaped by a particular context. Indeed, theological method for which the context is central rather than peripheral might be described broadly as *contextual*. As is the case with correlational method, the contextual approach can be construed as having several subcategories. A great deal of what is often described as "practical theology" occurs as a result of personal or communal *problem-solving*. Within a congregation, for example, the problem of boundary-setting occurs when the vestry or church council wrestles with what will be criteria for active voting membership. As communal discernment proceeds, theological questions are raised: What does it mean to be a member of the body of Christ? What does God expect (and therefore what should we expect) of a baptized believer and disciple of Jesus?

Another variation of contextual method that has gained increasing attention in recent years is carried out under the banner known as *public theology*. This theological method emanates from deep commitment to the conviction that true theology is not some kind of secretive code word for insiders, but public proclamation to be as understandable in the tumultuous public square by John D. Unbeliever as within the sanguine sanctuary by Jane C. Truebeliever.

A final theological method considered in this addendum (again, with this baker's dozen list of approaches understood as by no means exhaustive) might be described as deeply *communal*. Through the centuries, probably the bulk of theological work has been done by highly educated individuals closeted away in studies, monasteries, libraries, or remote summer cottages where professors spend extended sabbaticals writing their grand opuses. In more recent decades, again with pioneering efforts emerging out of liberationist and feminist impulses, theology has become a more communal enterprise. Recognizing that the church is a community or it is nothing, ecclesiastical or churchly theology is often becoming more dialogical; theological writings increasingly are coauthored books or anthologies by multiple writers in conversation with each other.

Notes

Preface

1. Thomas J. J. Altizer, *The Gospel of Christian Atheism* (Philadelphia: Westminster, 1966), 15.
2. Ibid., 26.
3. Serene Jones and Paul Lakeland, eds., *Constructive Theology: A Contemporary Approach to Classical Themes* (Minneapolis: Fortress Press, 2005), 4.
4. Karl Barth, *Evangelical Theology: An Introduction*, trans. Grover Foley (Garden City, N.Y.: Doubleday, Anchor Books ed., 1964), 35–36.

Chapter 1

1. Not all theologians are convinced that there is any personal dimension to the new age of resurrection reality. In pondering the question whether an individual "lives on" in any sense after physical death, Rosemary Radford Ruether, for example, concludes, "The appropriate response to these questions is an agnosticism. We should not pretend to know what we do not know." See Rosemary Radford Ruether, *Sexism and God-Talk: Toward a Feminist Theology* (Boston: Beacon, 1983), 257.
2. Many contemporary articulations of realized eschatology trace their roots to C. H. Dodd and his groundbreaking work on the parables. In *The Parables of Jesus* (1935), Dodd contends that at the core of Jesus'

teaching were eschatological declarations that the in-breaking of the kingdom of God had begun to occur.

3. Emil Brunner, *The Scandal of Christianity: The Gospel as Stumbling Block to Modern Man* (1951; repr., Atlanta: John Knox, 1981), 99–100. See also Oscar Cullmann, *Salvation in History* (New York: Harper & Row, 1967).
4. In every generation there are Christians who claim a high degree of certainty about the end-time and how and when it will come. Current fascination with the prospect of a cataclysmic rapture (in which true believers are suddenly swooped up into heaven as the torturous final days commence) is reflected in the popularity of such books as the best-selling Left Behind series by Tim LaHaye and Jerry Jenkins. A well-grounded biblical-theological probing of such current apocalyptic literature is offered by Barbara R. Rossing in *The Rapture Exposed: The Message of Hope in the Book of Revelation* (Boulder, Colo.: Westview, 2004).

Chapter 2

1. The first creation story appears in Genesis 1:1—2:4a, and a quite distinct second version appears in 2:4b-25.
2. Daniel L. Migliore, *Faith Seeking Understanding: An Introduction to Christian Theology* (Grand Rapids: Eerdmans, 2004), 115.
3. *The Confessions of St. Augustine*, bk. 11, chap. 12.
4. *Yahweh* is the common English rendering of YHWH, representing four Hebrew letters used by ancient God-fearers in place of the divine name so sacred it could not be written or uttered aloud.
5. Influenced heavily by the process philosophy of Alfred North Whitehead and others, process theology's key proponents have been scholars such as John Cobb, Charles Hartshorne, and Catherine Keller. For very readable introductions to process theology, see C. Robert Mesle's *Process Theology: A Basic Introduction* (St. Louis: Chalice, 1993) and "Process Theology" in James C. Livingston and Francis Schüssler Fiorenza, *Modern Christian Thought: The Twentieth Century* (Minneapolis: Fortress Press, 2006), 309–39.
6. See the catechism in any version of *The Book of Common Prayer*.
7. Robert Kolb and Timothy Wengert, eds. *The Book of Concord* (Minneapolis: Fortress Press, 2000), 433.
8. Karl Barth, *Church Dogmatics*, 2.2. *The Doctrine of God*, pt. 2, trans. G. W. Bromiley et al. (Edinburgh: T. & T. Clark, 1957), 413.

9. See Letty Russell, *The Future of Partnership* (Philadelphia: Westminster, 1979).
10. See Wolfhart Pannenberg, *What Is Man?* (Philadelphia: Fortress Press, 1970), 1–13.
11. Karl Rahner, *Theological Investigations II* (London: Darton, Longman & Todd, 1963), 240–41.
12. Joseph Sittler, *The Care of the Earth and Other University Sermons* (Philadelphia: Fortress Press, 1964), 97.
13. Sallie McFague, *A New Climate for Theology* (Minneapolis: Fortress Press, 2008), 86.

Chapter 3

1. Dietrich Bonhoeffer, *Life Together* (New York: Harper & Row, 1954), 27.
2. Saint Anselm is credited with the widely used definition of *theology* as "faith seeking understanding."
3. For an excellent summary of these and additional so-called theologies of liberation, see Susan Brooks Thistlethwaite and Mary Potter Engel, eds., *Lift Every Voice: Constructing Christian Theologies from the Underside* (Maryknoll, N.Y.: Orbis, 2004).
4. Numerous books and articles bear this phrase in their titles.
5. For an extended treatment of the concept of historical "threshold-crossing," see Robert Bacher and Michael Cooper-White, "Administration's Biography: A Holy History," in *Church Administration: Programs, Process, Purpose* (Minneapolis: Fortress Press, 2007), 1–23.
6. Stuart Sim, ed., *The Routledge Companion to Postmodernism* (London and New York: Routledge, 2002), vii. For another excellent succinct summary of postmodernism, see Pamela Cooper-White, *Shared Wisdom: The Use of the Self in Pastoral Care and Counseling* (Minneapolis: Augsburg Fortress, 2004), 36–43.
7. Included in Paul Tillich, *The Shaking of the Foundations* (New York: Scribner, 1948).
8. This terminology is associated particularly with the French philosophers Jacques Derrida and Michel Foucault, whose respective linguistic and sociopolitical critiques raised fundamental objections to the notion that one can conclude, "This is the way things are."
9. Matt Bai, "What Does It Take?" *New York Times Magazine*, July 15, 2007, 15–16.

10. Joseph A. Sittler, *Grace Notes and Other Fragments* (Philadelphia: Fortress Press, 1981), 24.
11. Thomas L. Friedman, *The World Is Flat: A Brief History of the Twenty-first Century* (New York: Ferrar, Straus and Giroux, 2006).
12. The Catechism of the Episcopal Church's *Book of Common Prayer* (New York: Oxford University Press, 1990) points to a version of general or *natural* revelation in the response to the question "How did God first help us?" "God first helped us by revealing himself and his will, through nature and history, through many seers and saints, and especially through the prophets of Israel" (BCP, 845).
13. This principle was first articulated by Anglican theologian Richard Hooker in the sixteenth century. For a more thorough explication, see www.episcopalchurch.org.
14. Robert Kolb and Timothy Wengert, eds. *The Book of Concord* (Minneapolis: Fortress Press, 2000), 355–56.
15. Work led by Finnish scholars (with Tuoma Manermaa as a key figure) has been significant in pondering the concept of *theosis* or "divinization." Not to be confused with salvation (which is pure gift by grace through faith), the process of sanctification (where humans may open ourselves through spiritual practices) can be the occasion for allowing God's further and deeper self-revelation.
16. Many theologians have spoken of God as "wholly Other," and also as "Holy Other." Perhaps the two twentieth-century theologians most associated with this terminology were Karl Barth and Rudolf Otto. See Karl Barth, *The Humanity of God*, trans. John N. Thomas and Thomas Weiser (Louisville: Westminster John Knox, 1960), and Rudolf Otto, *The Idea of the Holy: An Inquiry into the Non-rational Factor in the Idea of the Divine and Its Relation to the Rational,* trans. John W. Harvey (London: Oxford University Press, 1958).

Chapter 4

1. Biblical scholars continue to debate authorship and dating of the Hebrew Bible, with many (particularly the "textual critics") concluding that all portions can be dated within the first millennium BC, and others suggesting a period of perhaps fifteen hundred years or more.
2. For a succinct treatment of various types of biblical criticism, see John Barton, *Reading the Old Testament: Method in Biblical Study* (Philadel-

phia: Westminster, 1984). The *Catholic* and *Britannica* encyclopedias (including online versions) also offer good introductory articles.

3. Carl E. Braaten, "The Holy Scriptures," in *Christian Dogmatics,* ed. Carl E. Braaten and Robert W. Jenson (Philadelphia: Fortress Press, 1984), 1:63.
4. Ernst Käsemann, "The Canon of the New Testament and the Unity of the Church," in *Essays on New Testament Themes*, trans. W. J. Mantague (London: SCM, 1964).
5. The Evangelical Lutheran Church in America, for example, includes in each of its constitutions—for the church as a whole and for congregations and synods—the following Confession of Faith statement: "This church accepts the canonical Scriptures of the Old and New Testaments as the inspired Word of God and the authoritative source and norm of its proclamation, faith, and life." See *Constitutions, Bylaws and Continuing Resolutions of the Evangelical Lutheran Church in America.* From the Web site of the Evangelical Lutheran Church in America (www.elca.org).
6. "The Anglican approach to reading and interpreting the Bible was first articulated by Richard Hooker, also in the sixteenth century. While Christians universally acknowledge the Bible (or the Holy Scriptures) as the Word of God and completely sufficient to our reconciliation to God, what the Bible says must always speak to us in our own time and place. The church, as a worshiping body of faithful people, has for two thousand years amassed experience of God and of loving Jesus, and what they have said to us through the centuries about the Bible is critical to our understanding it in our own context. The traditions of the Church in interpreting Scripture connect all generations of believers together and give us a starting point for our own understanding. Episcopalians believe that every Christian must build an understanding and relationship with God's Word in the Bible, and to do that, God has given us intelligence and our own experience, which we refer to as 'Reason.' Based on the text of the Bible itself, and what Christians have taught us about it through the ages, we then must sort out our own understanding of it as it relates to our own lives." From the Web site of the Episcopal Church (www.ecusa.org).
7. Rudolf Bultmann et al., *Kerygma and Myth* (New York: Harper & Row, 1961).
8. Claudia Tikkun Setzer, "The Historical Jesus," in *Tikkun Magazine: A Bimonthly Critique of Politics, Culture and Society* 10, no. 4 (July 17, 1995): 73ff.

9. When the Lutheran World Federation, for example, declared apartheid in South Africa a matter of *status confessionis* (insisting that maintaining such an institutionalized manifestation of racism is utterly incompatible with the gospel and a matter of outright heresy), churches that did not join in its opposition were effectively "excommunicated" from the global Lutheran communion for a period of years.
10. Along with differing ways of interpreting the Bible and Lutheran Confessions, one of the key barriers to U.S. Lutheran unity between the Lutheran Church–Missouri Synod and Evangelical Lutheran Church in America is that the latter ordains women while the LC–MS continues to preclude female pastors. In the Episcopal Church and Anglican Communion, opposition to women's ordination continues to be divisive in some quarters as well.
11. See, for example, Martti Nissinen, *Homoeroticism in the Biblical World*, trans. Kirsi Stjerna (Minneapolis: Fortress Press, 1998); and Craig L. Nessan, *Many Members Yet One Body* (Minneapolis: Augsburg Fortress, 2004).

Chapter 5

1. Lyric excerpt from "Three Times a Lady" by Lionel Richie (Jobete Music, Inc., 1978).
2. The phrase has been attributed to Martin Luther and various other theologians in describing the challenging work of describing the Trinity.
3. Robert W. Jenson, "The Triune God," in *Christian Dogmatics*, ed. Carl E. Braaten and Robert W. Jenson, vol. 1 (Philadelphia: Fortress Press, 1977), 89.
4. Lyric excerpt from stanza 1 of "God Who Made the Earth and Heaven" by Reginald Heber, 1783–1826.
5. Lyric excerpt from "God, Who Stretched the Spangled Heavens" by Catherine Cameron (copyright © Hope Publishing Company, 1967).
6. Lyric excerpt from "God, Whose Farm Is All Creation" by John Arlott (copyright © Trustees of the late John Arlott).
7. Lyric excerpt from "God, My Lord, My Strength" by Jaroslav Vajda (copyright © Concordia Publishing House, 1969).
8. Lyric excerpt from "God of the Sparrow" by Jaroslav Vajda (copyright © Concordia Publishing House, 1983).
9. Lyric excerpt from "O God, My Faithful God" by Catherine Winkworth, 1827–1878.

10. Duane H. Larson, "Ministry from Word and Sacrament: A Diaconal Ministry Theology," in *From Word and Sacrament: Renewed Vision for Diaconal Ministry*, ed. Duane H. Larson (Chicago: Evangelical Lutheran Church in America, 1999), 113.
11. Braaten and Jenson, *Christian Dogmatics*, 1:138.
12. Jürgen Moltmann, *Theology of Hope* (Minneapolis: Fortress Press, 1993), 141.
13. Elizabeth A. Johnson, *She Who Is: The Mystery of God in Feminist Theological Discourse* (New York: Crossroad, 1999), 192–93.
14. For an articulate and well-reasoned challenge to the assertion that Father, Son, Holy Spirit is God's "'Name' and therefore liturgically indispensable," see Susan Brooks Thistlethwaite, "On the Trinity," in *Lift Every Voice: Constructing Christian Theologies from the Underside,* ed. Susan Brooks Thistlethwaite and Mary Potters Engel (Maryknoll, N.Y.: Orbis, 2004), 121ff.
15. The Conference of Bishops of the Evangelical Lutheran Church in America, for example, issued a word of pastoral advice in 1991 affirming use of the traditional trinitarian language in baptism: " 'In the name of the Father, and of the Son, and of the Holy Spirit' is therefore the only doctrinally acceptable way for a person to be baptized into the Body of Christ. The Gospel promises that in Baptism we are graciously united by the Spirit into the death and resurrection of Jesus Christ, with whom we too may then address God confidently as 'our Father.' This view fulfills the apostolic understanding of our risen Lord's commission for the Church to practice a Trinitarian Baptism in Matthew 28. It is also faithfully reflected in the Trinitarian baptismal formula pronounced by the Church throughout the ages, as presented in the rite for Holy Baptism in the Lutheran Book of Worship" (www.elca.org/synods/bishopstrinitarian).
16. Helpful guidelines for the use of inclusive language are available from many sources. See, for example, recommended bias-free terminology cited in the *Publishing Standards Manual* of the Evangelical Lutheran Church in America (www.elca.org/officeofthesecretary).
17. Rublev's icon is widely available in books of religious art, as well as on the Internet.
18. Pamela Cooper-White, *Many Voices: Pastoral Psychotherapy in Relational and Theological Perspective* (Minneapolis: Fortress Press, 2007), 81.
19. "Come, Join the Dance of the Trinity," by Richard Leach, © 2001 Selah Publishing Co., Inc., www.selahpub.com. All rights reserved. Used by permission.

Chapter 6

1. The most prominent false Christological teaching or "heresy" was that attributed to Arius, who denied Jesus' full divinity and taught that the Son was indeed created by the Father. Of Jesus, Arius stated, "There was [a time] when he was not."
2. For a thorough treatment of these issues and a summary of Chalcedon, see Bradley C. Hanson, *Introduction to Christian Theology* (Minneapolis: Fortress Press, 1997), 144–47; also Daniel L. Migliore, *Faith Seeking Understanding: An Introduction to Christian Theology* (Grand Rapids: Eerdmans, 2004), 169–82.
3. Dietrich Bonhoeffer, *Letters and Papers from Prison*, ed. Eberhard Bethge (New York: Macmillan, 1972), 361.
4. Article III of the Augsburg Confession, in *The Book of Concord: The Confessions of the Evangelical Lutheran Church*, ed. Robert Kolb and Timothy J. Wengert (Minneapolis: Fortress Press, 2000), 39.
5. This theory/image of the atonement as Christ triumphing over the forces of evil and "winning humans back for God" gained renewed attention with the 1931 publication of Swiss bishop Gustaf Aulen's *Christus Victor: An Historical Study of the Three Main Types of the Idea of Atonement*. Multiple later editions of the classic work have been published and are widely available.
6. Lisa Isherwood, *Introducing Feminist Christologies* (Cleveland: Pilgrim, 2002), 31.
7. Carter Heyward, "Jesus of Nazareth/Christ of Faith: Foundations for a Reactive Christology," in *Lift Every Voice: Constructing Christian Theologies from the Underside*, ed. Susan Brooks Thistlethwaite and Mary Potter Engle (Maryknoll, N.Y.: Orbis, 2004), 198.
8. James H. Cone, "God Is Black," in Thistlethwaite and Engle, *Lift Every Voice*, 101.
9. Elsa Tamez, *The Amnesty of Grace: Justification by Faith from a Latin American Perspective*, trans. Sharon H. Ringe (Nashville: Abingdon, 1993), 134.
10. Sidney Norton Deane, trans., *St. Anselm*, 2.6 (LaSalle, Ill.: Open Court, 1903), 173ff.
11. Jürgen Moltmann, *The Crucified God* (Minneapolis: Fortress Press, 1973), 37.
12. Paul Tillich, *The Shaking of the Foundations* (New York: Scribner, 1948), 161–62.

13. Douglas John Hall, *Lighten Our Darkness: Toward an Indigenous Theology of the Cross* (Philadelphia: Westminster, 1976), 117.
14. The biblical teaching articulated most clearly by Paul in Romans is explicated in a multitude of books, articles, and theological treatises. Among the most succinct and broadly influential statements on justification is Article IV of the Augsburg Confession, which receives more expansive treatment in the *Apology.* For the most recent English translations, see Kolb and Wengert, *Book of Concord.*
15. Joint Declaration on the Doctrine of Justification by the Lutheran World Federation and the Catholic Church, paras. 18 and 25; available at www.lutheranworld.org and http://vatican.va/roman.
16. The so-called longer ending of Mark's gospel found in some texts and manuscripts also speaks of Jesus' being "taken up into heaven," where he "sat down at the right hand of God" (Mark 16:19-20).

Chapter 7

1. "The Church of Christ, in Every Age," text by Fred Pratt Green, 1903–2000; copyright © 1971 Hope Publishing Company, Carol Stream, IL 60188. All rights reserved. Used by permission.
2. While it goes beyond the scope of this book to offer an in-depth explanation, the so-called *filioque* controversy should simply be noted. This phrase within the Nicene Creed's third article has been rendered differently in the Western church since the sixth century when in the West "and the Son" was added to the original "proceeds from the Father." Until recent dialogues achieved breakthroughs, this creedal divergence was a chief point of controversy between Western Christianity and Eastern Orthodoxy.
3. For a more complete discussion of "the appropriateness of using female imagery of the Spirit," see Daniel L. Migliore, *Faith Seeking Understanding: An Introduction to Christian Theology*, 2nd ed. (Grand Rapids: Eerdmans, 2004), 233–34.
4. Robert Kolb and Timothy J. Wengert, eds., *The Book of Concord: The Confessions of the Evangelical Lutheran Church* (Minneapolis: Fortress Press, 2000), 355–56.
5. Ted Peters, *God—the World's Future* (Minneapolis: Fortress Press, 1992), 247.

6. In a classic little book called *Images of the Church in the New Testament*, Paul Minear cited no fewer than ninety-six biblical images used for the church (Philadelphia: Westminster, 1960).
7. Martin Luther, "First Sunday in Advent" (Church Postil, 1522), in *Sermons of Martin Luther*, ed. John Nicholas Lenker, vol. 1 (1905; repr., Grand Rapids: Baker, 1988), 44. (For the original, see Luther, Martin. *D. Martin Luthers Werke, Kritische Gesamtausgabe.* (Weimar: Verlag Hermann Böhlaus Nochfolger, 1883–), 10(1):2.
8. The Augsburg Confession, Article VII, in Kolb and Wengert, *Book of Concord*, 42.
9. See *The Book of Common Prayer* (New York: Church Publishing, 1979).
10. *Luther's Works*, American ed. (Philadelphia: Muhlenberg; and St. Louis: Concordia, 1967), 44:240.
11. Philip J. Hefner, "The Church and the Kingdom of God," in *Christian Dogmatics*, ed. Carl E. Braaten and Robert W. Jenson (Philadelphia: Fortress Press, 1984), 2:246–47.
12. Migliore, *Faith Seeking Understanding*, 252.

Chapter 8

1. "You Satisfy the Hungry Heart" by Omer Westendorf, © 1977 Archdiocese of Philadelphia.
2. See "An Outline of the Faith, Commonly Called the Catechism," in *The Book of Common Prayer* (New York: Church Publishing, 1979).
3. Robert Kolb and Timothy J. Wengert, eds., *The Book of Concord: The Confessions of the Evangelical Lutheran Church* (Minneapolis: Fortress Press, 2000), 219.
4. Augustine, *In Johannem*, 80.3.
5. Robert W. Jenson, *Visible Words* (Philadelphia: Fortress Press, 1978), 3.
6. Daniel L. Migliore, *Faith Seeking Understanding: An Introduction to Christian Theology* (Grand Rapids: Eerdmans, 2004), 280.
7. In keeping with its classic self-definition as offering a *via media*, or "middle way," the Episcopal/Anglican Church, in its catechism, regards these five as "other sacramental rites."
8. Kolb and Wengert, *Book of Concord*, 359.
9. Jenson, *Visible Words*, 148.
10. Justo Gonzalez and Zaida Maldonado Perez, *An Introduction to Christian Theology* (Nashville: Abingdon, 2002), 130.

11. Gordon W. Lathrop, *Holy Things: A Liturgical Theology* (Minneapolis: Fortress Press, 1993), 165.
12. See "An Outline of the Faith, Commonly Called the Catechism."
13. Westminster Catechism, question 168.
14. Kolb and Wengert, *Book of Concord*, 362.
15. Ibid.
16. Bradley C. Hanson, *Introduction to Christian Theology* (Minneapolis: Fortress Press, 1997), 279.
17. *Baptism, Eucharist and Ministry: Faith and Order Paper #111* (World Council of Churches, 1982), "Eucharist," Section IIE, #26.

Chapter 9

1. *Baptism, Eucharist and Ministry, Faith and Order Paper* 111 (World Council of Churches, 1982), "Ministry," Section I.5.
2. See Martin Luther's treatise *On the Freedom of a Christian*: "Christ has made it possible for us to be not only his brethren, co-heirs, and fellow-kings, but also his fellow-priests."
3. Ibid.
4. Philip J. Hefner, "Basic Elements of the Church's Life," in *Christian Dogmatics*, ed. Carl E. Braaten and Robert W. Jenson (Minneapolis: Fortress Press, 1984), 2:224–26.
5. I was first introduced to this phrase by my seminary homiletics teacher, Dr. Herman G. Stuempfle. It has been attributed to many, including theologian Wayne Meeks.
6. Gordon W. Lathrop, *Holy Things: A Liturgical Theology* (Minneapolis: Fortress Press, 1993), 185.
7. See, for example, *Constitution, Bylaws and Continuing Resolutions of the Evangelical Lutheran Church in America* (latest version available at www.elca.org), which states (7.31.11): "Persons admitted to and continued in the ordained ministry of this church shall satisfactorily meet and maintain the following:
    a. commitment to Christ;
    b. acceptance of and adherence to the Confession of Faith of this church;
    c. willingness and ability to serve in response to the needs of this church;
    d. academic and practical qualifications for ministry, including leadership abilities and competence in interpersonal relationships;

e. commitment to lead a life worthy of the Gospel of Christ and in so doing to be an example in faithful service and holy living;
f. receipt and acceptance of a letter of call; and
g. membership in a congregation of this church."

8. Eric Gritsch, *Fortress Introduction to Lutheranism* (Minneapolis: Fortress Press, 1994), 114–15.
9. *Evangelical Lutheran Worship* (Minneapolis: Augsburg Fortress, 2006), 94.

Chapter 10

1. Letty Russell, *The Future of Partnership* (Philadelphia: Westminster, 1979), 102.
2. Text © 1978 *Lutheran Book of Worship*, admin. Augsburg Fortress and music © 2006 Augsburg Fortress.
3. Kathryn Tanner, *Jesus, Humanity and the Trinity: A Brief Systematic Theology* (Minneapolis: Fortress Press, 2001), 67–68.
4. Creation-centered ethics typically includes extended treatment of the concept of *natural law*, the assertion that woven into the very fabric of creation (and especially of us human created ones) are fundamental norms and knowledge of good and evil, right and wrong behavior. While natural law ethical perspectives have been espoused most frequently and articulately within the Roman Catholic tradition, so-called Protestants should also give serious consideration to them. For a brief thorough treatment of the topic, see Carl E. Braaten, "Reclaiming the Natural Law for Theological Ethics," in online *Journal of Lutheran Ethics* (www.elca.org/jle).
5. *Heidelberg Disputation* no. 20.
6. I am indebted to Rev. Steven Ullestad, currently bishop of the Northeastern Iowa Synod of the Evangelical Lutheran Church in America, for voicing this suggestion of an appropriate stance for those who uphold a cruciform ethics.
7. See the social statement "Church in Society: A Lutheran Perspective" (Evangelical Lutheran Church in America, 8765 W. Higgins Road, Chicago, IL 60631 or www.elca.org/socialstatements).
8. A comprehensive overview of five basic approaches to Christian ethical relationship to and involvement in society is provided in H. Richard Niebuhr, *Christ and Culture* (New York: Harper & Row, 1951).

9. Gerhard O. Forde, "Justification and This World," *Church Dogmatics*, ed. Carl E. Braaten and Robert W. Jenson, vol. 2 (Minneapolis: Fortress Press, 1984), 458.
10. Martin Luther, for example, held in high regard civil authorities (as long as they did not infringe on the freedom of Christians), was vociferous in denouncing radical "revolutionaries" of his time, and deemed as "prophet, priest, servant and teacher" all who served in the civic realm "as pious jurists," meaning "the whole profession, including chancellors, secretaries, judges, advocates, notaries, and all who have to do with the legal side of government" (*Luther's Works*, vol. 44, American ed. [Philadelphia: Muhlenberg; and St. Louis: Concordia, 1967], 240).
11. See the lively discussion of how "the church" must call to account "the state" when the latter oversteps its bounds in Helmut Thielicke, *Theological Ethics*, vol. 2 (Philadelphia: Fortress Press, 1969). Thielicke speaks of "eschatological relativization" in asserting that the claims of the state are always penultimate and must be judged over against mandates flowing from the gospel (p. 251). For another in-depth consideration of church-state relations, see Karl Barth, *Community, Church and State* (New York: Anchor Books, 1960).
12. Bonhoeffer's autobiographical reflection in *Letters and Papers from Prison* (available in multiple versions) is a compelling testimony from this twentieth-century Christian widely regarded as a martyr.
13. Romero's life story and some of his powerful sermons are available from multiple sources, including many materials now posted on various Web sites. For two excellent introductory works, see James R. Brockman, *Romero: A Life* (Maryknoll, N.Y.: Orbis, 1989), and Brockman's translated version of Romero's *The Violence of Love* (New York: Harper & Row, 1988). In his final homily, at the conclusion of which shots rang out and the bishop was mortally wounded, Romero declared (on March 24, 1980): "God's reign is already present on our earth in mystery. When the Lord comes, it will be brought to perfection. That is the hope that inspires Christians. We know that every effort to better society, especially when injustice and sin are so ingrained, is an effort that God blesses, that God wants, that God demands of us."
14. A variety of resources and training institutes (some of which have been called "Schools for Discernmentarians") has been developed recently. See, for example, Charles M. Olsen, *Transforming Church Boards into Communities of Spiritual Leaders* (Herndon, Va.: Alban, 1995), and

Danny E. Morris and Charles M. Olsen, *Discerning God's Will Together: A Spiritual Practice for the Church* (Herndon, Va.: Alban, 1997).

15. Susan Brooks Thistlethwaite and Mary Potter Engle, eds., *Lift Every Voice: Constructing Christian Theologies from the Underside* (Maryknoll, N.Y.: Orbis, 2004), 8.

Postscript

1. Church historian and prolific author Martin Marty has often used this image of "grave-merry Christians," and I am indebted to both Marty and Hugo Rahner for the phrase.
2. Dr. Lawrence Folkemer, professor emeritus of systematic theology at the Lutheran Theological Seminary at Gettysburg, used this phrase in a lecture on eschatology during the introductory theology course my first year in seminary, 1972–73.
3. Robert W. Jenson, *A Large Catechism* (Delhi, N.Y.: American Lutheran Publicity Bureau, 1999), 8.

Addendum

1. Daniel L. Migliore, *Faith Seeking Understanding: An Introduction to Christian Theology* (Grand Rapids: Eerdmans, 2004), 16.
2. Ibid., 16.
3. Donald G. Luck, *Why Study Theology?* (St. Louis: Chalice, 1999), 115.
4. For the most recent English translation, see Robert Kolb and Timothy J. Wengert, eds., *The Book of Concord: The Confessions of the Evangelical Lutheran Church* (Minneapolis: Fortress Press, 2000).
5. Paul Tillich, *Systematic Theology,* vol. 1 (University of Chicago Press, 1951), 30, 60–64.
6. In chapter 4 of their brief introductory book, *How to Think Theologically* (Minneapolis: Fortress Press, 1996), Howard W. Stone and James O. Duke offer another perspective on correlational theology, noting that its starting point may be either primarily *anthropological* (whereby a theologian will "look first at Christian faith in the context of human living") or *revelatory* (in which the theologians "begin by focusing on the message of God as revealed in Scripture").

Index